Retirement for Workaholics

Retirement for Workaholics

Life after Work in a Downsized Economy

MORLEY D. GLICKEN

 PRAEGER

AN IMPRINT OF ABC-CLIO, LLC
Santa Barbara, California • Denver, Colorado • Oxford, England

Copyright 2010 by Morley D. Glicken

All rights reserved. No part of this publication may be reproduced, stored in a
retrieval system, or transmitted, in any form or by any means, electronic,
mechanical, photocopying, recording, or otherwise, except for the inclusion of
brief quotations in a review, without prior permission in writing from the publisher.

Library of Congress Cataloging-in-Publication Data

Glicken, Morley D.
  Retirement for workaholics : life after work in a downsized economy /
Morley D. Glicken.
    p. cm.
  Includes bibliographical references and index.
  ISBN 978-0-313-38486-8 (hbk. : alk. paper) — ISBN 978-0-313-38487-5 (ebook)
1. Workaholics—Retirement. 2. Retirement—Planning. I. Title.
  HQ1062.G547 2010
  155.2'32—dc22   2010002198

ISBN: 978-0-313-38486-8
EISBN: 978-0-313-38487-5

14 13 12 11 10   1 2 3 4 5

This book is also available on the World Wide Web as an eBook.
Visit www.abc-clio.com for details.

Praeger
An Imprint of ABC-CLIO, LLC

ABC-CLIO, LLC
130 Cremona Drive, P.O. Box 1911
Santa Barbara, California 93116-1911

This book is printed on acid-free paper ∞

Manufactured in the United States of America

Contents

Preface

Like me, many of you have worked very hard at jobs that have given you pleasure. It's not easy to think about retirement when so much of your life has been spent working. Even though you may have other interests, stopping work because you've been downsized or because you're, quite frankly, burned out isn't easy, particularly if you've neglected other areas of your life and now find yourself without the pleasures of a rich family life and outside interests when you have the free time that retirement provides.

This is a book for those of you who need some help in approaching retirement even though you haven't taken the time to plan or develop some of the skills necessary to retire happily. It needn't be a time without work, and as a dedicated but happy workaholic, I'm aware of how silly and unusable many retirement books are because they aren't really geared to the type of person you are and are likely to continue to be once you retire.

In chapter 1, I go into detail about what the book contains and how it can be of help to you and your family. As an academic and mental health professional, but also as a 69-year-old man who knows a lot about the complexities of retirement, I want to offer you information grounded in the realities of age, experience, and research on workaholism and retirement. I also want to include stories from workaholics I know explaining how they transitioned into retirement after years of mind-numbing work at the expense of personal happiness and family life.

I hope you will find this book helpful, and although I use the terms *work-aholic* and *work-addicted*, I don't want to characterize anyone who works hard as dysfunctional. We make the world work, and without us, nothing would get done.

Morley D. Glicken
Prescott, Arizona

PART I

Understanding Work-Addicted Behavior

Chapters 1 through 4 will help you better understand work addictions and why they create health and emotional problems. Also covered are the distinctions between hard workers and workaholics, or what I prefer to call work-addicted people. Work addictions have a number of causes, and as you will discover in the coming chapters, there are a number of different types of workaholics.

Chapter 1 is an introduction to workaholism and to the book. Chapter 2 describes, in some detail, the characteristics of work-addicted people. Chapter 3 discusses the physical and emotional impact of work-addicted behavior, while chapter 4 provides the 10 irrational ideas behind workaholism and what can be done to change them.

In the following chapters, I will also provide personal stories written by friends and colleagues who consider themselves hard workers and who, at times, have dealt with work addictions for a variety of reasons. Their insights into their behavior and the ways in which they have moved into retirement will, hopefully be helpful to many of you who are also moving—not happily, perhaps—toward retirement, often because the economy has given you no choice.

CHAPTER 1

Introduction: Hard Worker or Workaholic?

Americans are hard workers. Many of us put in much more than 40 hours of work each week. It's not unusual for us to take work home with us, to work during vacation time, and not to feel in the least that what we're doing is somehow a problem. But for some older adults who are truly work addicted, retirement can be a nightmare without work to keep us occupied. How can we go from working 50- to 60-hour weeks, and more, into retirement, where there's a chance that we might have little to keep us occupied? That's what this book is about. For those of you who have worked harder than most people (you can call us work addicted, or workaholics, or very, very hard workers), life without work can seem pretty awful.

Unfortunately, the new economy has forced many older workers to leave jobs before they've had a chance to plan for retirement. Many of them have limited ability to deal with leisure time and dread the thought of retirement even when they're completely burned out at their current jobs. Others, who work 60 to 80 hours a week but have health problems and need to cut back or take early retirement, often have difficulty dealing with unscheduled and unproductive time. Although we may call these workers workaholics or work addicted, the fact is that they have lives built around work and now face the last third of their lives searching for ways to stay busy and replicate the schedules and projects they had when they were employed.

This book is written as a practical guide for people who invest their lives in work and often have limited outside interests. Your author is a 69-year-old university professor and mental health professional who considers himself a workaholic and has grappled with many of the same problems you are grappling with as you move from full-time work to retirement. The book discusses the latest research on workaholics and retirement and includes personal stories from hardworking colleagues and friends who have successfully dealt with retirement after years of giving their all to work. The book has the following objectives:

1. It will help the reader understand the difference between people who are hardworking but have rich personal lives and workaholics who are work addicted and often lack fulfilling personal lives.

2. It will help you understand the very real health problems associated with work addictions and the risk of those health problems worsening as you age.

3. The book will point out the impact of work addiction on marriages, families, and friendships. Work addiction can be very lonely and isolating.

4. The book will help you recognize that being work addicted isn't always a negative and that it can be used to maintain physical and emotional health in retirement with appropriate projects, constructive use of leisure time, and work-related activities that will be discussed in detail in the book.

5. If you were forced out of work or downsized, the book will help you deal with your negative feelings toward those responsible.

6. It will help you understand that burnout doesn't mean you're burned up on work and that other opportunities are available, even in a bad economy, that can make retirement a positive experience.

7. The book includes the most current research on retirement and the impact it has on workaholics, and provides research-supported strategies to improve satisfaction with retirement.

8. The book will show, through many actual stories of hardworking, sometimes work-addicted older people that retirement doesn't mean that you'll stop working. Quite the contrary, it means that you can work on projects that really excite you.

9. Of all retirees, workaholics most often put off retirement planning and are frequently ill-prepared for life without work. The book will explain how workaholics can use their abilities to plan a successful and satisfying retirement.

10. The book will help you recognize that millions of retirees enjoy the opportunity to combine work with leisure time, travel, and physical activity not available while they worked full-time.

11. The book offers stories from work-addicted retirees about their initial problems with retirement and the creative ways they've gone about transitioning from all-consuming work to happy and successful retired life.

THE DIFFERENCE BETWEEN HARDWORKING PEOPLE AND WORKAHOLICS

Before I started researching this book, I thought I knew what a workaholic was: someone who works so much that nothing else matters. Workaholics, I thought, were work-addicted people who have no other interests than work and who work to the detriment of family, loved ones, and anything else that matters to many of us. And pity the older workaholic with retirement looming who has no idea how to use free, unscheduled time and who now dreads the idea of life without work.

That certainly is one definition of *workaholism*, but it's not the only one. For many hardworking men and women, life without work is tough. Many of us get great joy out of our work. We experience status and financial rewards from our labors. We create, and build, and make our dreams come true. Why shouldn't we work hard, and why shouldn't we feel ambivalent about retirement if it means a great deal of spare time to do things we never wanted to do when we were working and that we certainly don't want to do in retirement?

Linn (2009) reports that a combination of good health, inability to deal with spare time, continued interest in their jobs, economic necessity, and the other rewards of work are pushing some Americans to stay in the workforce long past traditional retirement age. About 7 percent of people aged 75 or older were in the labor force as of June 2009, up from about 5 percent a decade ago. That translates into more than 1.1 million people working past age 74, up from 750,000 a decade ago.

But given the economy, many of us who get joy out of work are being downsized and experience the ageism of the workplace that often lets older workers go because they cost more. Forget about our value to an organization, hard work, and loyalty; the reality is that many of us are removed from the work we love, not because we can't cut it anymore, but because we are expendable.

What should we do and how can we occupy ourselves in a job market where old is anyone over 50 and what we accomplished in the past doesn't matter? And how can we better understand our need to work and channel it productively so that what we love doing doesn't end up in depression once it's taken away? Furthermore, how can we understand our behavior better and use it creatively if we are forced to retire or if work truly is an addiction?

As someone who still works very hard, is a bit compulsive like many of you, and qualifies as an older adult (69 when this book was written), I think that work is good and that the people who do it with love and commitment are the best. So let's start out with an understanding that this book isn't intended to insult you with simplistic notions about who you are or why you are that way. It's about making the most of the positive attributes you bring into retirement—forced, voluntary, or otherwise.

UNDERSTANDING THE CONCEPT OF WORK ADDICTION

I want to clarify the difference between positive work addiction and unhealthy work addiction, or workaholism. Let me start out with the negative view of workaholics. *Workaholism* can be defined as valuing work over any other activity when, and this is important, it affects your physical and emotional health; the quality of your work; and your family, spouse, and children. There are a number of very hardworking people who put in long hours, but when they're free, they give back to their loved ones and enjoy relationships and outside activities. When work becomes all consuming and joyless—that is, you do it but you go well beyond what is necessary to do the job well and have no other interests or activities beyond work—we might then call it a negative addiction. You do it because you have nothing else to take its place. Without constant work, you know that you'll become anxious and depressed. A negative work addiction is a constant and recurring obsession with joyless work.

It's true that many aspects of work are joyless and unpleasant, but we put up with them by getting pleasure from other aspects of the job and from our outside activities and loved ones. Also, in this down economy, many people work hard to keep their jobs. I don't want to call these people work addicted when they are just trying to survive. Real workaholics have few if any outside interests. They let family life fall apart. They often have health problems and suffer from depression and deep insecurity. Like any addiction, they repeat behaviors that are destructive even though they know it. They would like to stop, but like all real addictions, they find stopping difficult to impossible.

But as Stein (2009) reminds us, work addicts should not be confused with people who are simply hard workers, love their work, and go the extra mile to finish a project. By contrast, workaholics constantly think about work and without work feel anxious and depressed. They're often difficult to get along with and push others as hard as they push themselves.

Saul (2009) suggests the following differences between hard workers and workaholics:

1. Hard workers think of work as a required and, at times, a pleasurable obligation. Workaholics see work as a way to distance themselves from unwanted feelings and relationships.

2. Hard workers keep work in check so that they can be available to their family and friends. Workaholics believe that work is more important than anything else in their lives, including family and friends.

3. Workaholics get excitement from meeting impossible demands. Hard workers do not.

4. Hard workers can take breaks from work, while workaholics cannot. They think about work regardless of what they're doing or who they're with. (p. 1)

An interesting way of understanding the difference between hard workers and workaholics is found in the research of Douglas and Morris (2006), who believe that what we typically call a workaholic, with its negative connotations, may more correctly be understood when we look at that person's motivation to work. The researchers found that people work hard for four reasons. First, there are people who work hard because they want the financial rewards of hard work. Douglas and Morris call these people hard workers who are *material goal seekers*. Others work long hours because they find little enjoyment from leisure activities—they might better be called *low-leisure hard workers*. Still others work a great deal because they love the perks and might more reasonably be called *perkaholics* rather than workaholics. Perks are the intangibles of work and might include friendships, an easy commute to work, great working conditions, a good health plan, and so on. Finally, there are those who work long hours for its own sake—these people might properly be called *workaholics*.

I would add a fifth type of motivation, and that's people who work a great deal because they simply love what they're doing. I know many university professors who can't wait to work on projects when they get up in the morning. They have a love affair with the work they do and consider it a blessing to have the time and support to work on special projects in addition to their teaching responsibilities. The average university professor works 55 hours a week. This isn't to say that some of them aren't workaholics with the many problems that come with work addictions. However, most of them love their jobs and work for salaries far below what they could make in the business world. Many of them continue to work full-time or part-time well beyond normal retirement age, not for the money or because they need to stay busy, but because they love what they're doing, and leaving the academic life would be unthinkable.

Personal Story: On the Joys of Being an Older Published Author

"I recently attended a lecture by my well-known fellow writer Christopher Hitchens. I count Mr. Hitchens as a colleague because I've published 12 books in the past six years, although my students think the North Dakota Ollie and Lena jokes I include in all my books are the best part of them.

"Mr. Hitchens was brilliant and entertaining. I could probably learn a lot from him about being a successful writer such as wearing a white suit, drinking wine during the lecture, using words that would make my sainted mother blush, and fingering a cigarette so longingly that even though I don't smoke, I wanted to grab it out of his hand and smoke it for him.

"I've been writing books for the past few years since I retired from full-time teaching, and retired or not, the truth is that I put my heart and soul into my books. I never care how many I sell or whether I make any money. I write to please myself. I have a book that came out in 2009 about older adults that makes me proud when I read it. I'm almost done with a mystery novel set in my hometown of Grand Forks, North Dakota, with descriptions of the weather that no one believes and stories about my friends and teachers in Grand Forks that make people envious and question my memory. 'Was it really that magical?' they ask. Yes, yes it was.

"One of my books is about men, but it's really about my father and the tough and tender immigrant people with whom I grew up in North Dakota. Another book is about psychological resilience, but it's really about my daughter and members of my family who struggle with illness and every imaginable setback and yet come out of that struggle stronger than ever. Another book is about positive psychology, an approach to helping others that focuses on what's right about people. I wrote it in the mountains of Utah where every day, deer and moose would come to my door and watch me write. No one could ever put a dollar value on that special experience.

"My daughter Amy has contributed to many of my books. This is what she wrote about her juvenile-onset diabetes: 'After having diabetes for 14 years, it has become more than a chronic disease for me, more than a steady companion; diabetes is very much a part of who I am. Diabetes is not a burden, nor is it a crutch. It is just a disease that I, and millions of others, live with every moment of every day. I live with diabetes as though it were my troubled child—a lot of work and occasionally painful, but in the end, oddly beautiful and uniquely mine.' Who wouldn't want to write books when you can include such beauty?

"I live in the mountains of Arizona near Sedona—paradise. We have mesquite trees, lush desert vegetation, and a waterfall and pond in our backyard. Deer, owls, hawks, javelina, bobcats, raccoons, and more varieties of birds than I can describe come to the pond to drink. As I look out every morning before I write, the one thing I can say that perhaps Mr. Hitchens can't is that I feel blessed to be able to do what I've always wanted to do: to be a published writer and to understand, in my daughter's words, that our task 'is simply to discern what our gifts are and to utilize them. Because, in the end, we are each our own Tooth Fairy, taking what has been lost and giving gold in return.'"—MDG

SUMMARY

This chapter made an important distinction between hard workers and workaholics. Many of us work hard, but work isn't the totality of our lives. Workaholics push personal relationships aside and focus on work because it's often their way of protecting themselves from relationships and life experiences that make them uncomfortable and require skills they lack. A personal story written by the author describes the joy he gets from writing and how retirement has given him the time to write and to appreciate nature, the beauty of the Arizona mountains, and his family.

REFERENCES

Douglas, E.J., & Morris, R.L. (2006). Workaholic, or just hard worker? *Career Development International, 11*, 394–417.

Linn, A. (2009, July 29). *When the golden years include a commute: Some are opting to work into their 70s, 80s and beyond.* Retrieved August 3, 2009, from http://www.msnbc.msn.com/id/32089674/ns/business-personal_finance.

Saul, T. T. (2009). *Being a hard worker vs. being a workaholic.* Retrieved August 12, 2009, from http://www.saulandsaul.com/resources/BEING+A+HARD+WORKER+VS+BEING+A+WORKAHOLIC.pdf.

Stein, L. (2009). *Workaholism.* Retrieved August 12, 2009, from http://www.aheal thyme.com/topic/workaholism.

CHAPTER 2

Descriptions of Workaholics

Griffiths (2005) writes that "the most obvious sign that someone is a workaholic is when work and work-related concerns preoccupy a person's life to the neglect of everything else in it. What starts out as love of work can often end up with the person developing perfectionist, then obsessional traits" (p. 97).

According to Machlowitz (1980), workaholics share six traits: they (1) are intense, energetic, competitive, and driven; (2) have self-doubts; (3) prefer work to leisure; (4) work anytime, anywhere; (5) make the most of their time; and (6) blur the distinction between business and pleasure. As a consequence, it is not uncommon for workaholics to have major health problems, including stress-induced illnesses, chronic fatigue, and increased anxiety levels.

A number of researchers have noted that many people who work hard and are very likely workaholics have few if any of the emotional problems associated with workaholism. The term *enthusiastic workaholics* is used to describe workaholics without health problems who learn the requirements of a job quickly, excel at their work, put great amounts of time into the job, and reap the rewards for their efforts. *Nonenthusiastic workaholics*, who have health risks, put a great deal of time and effort into work but are given none of the rewards associated with hard work. Many of these people work in organizations without systems for rewarding exceptional work effort or that have internal biases against certain types of workers (e.g., women, people of color, workers of a certain age, and people without formal education who nonetheless work very hard and contribute).

In chapter 1, I mentioned Douglas and Morris's (2006) work about motivation to work as a better way of separating people who work hard but are not workaholics from people who most certainly are. But what about type A personalities, those hard-driving, erasable people we commonly associate with being workaholics? Are they truly workaholics? Friedman and Rosenman (1974) indicate that type A personalities are impatient, time conscious, concerned about their status, highly competitive, ambitious, businesslike, and aggressive and have difficulty relaxing. Furthermore, they are often high-achieving workaholics who drive themselves with deadlines and are unhappy about delays. Because of these characteristics, type A individuals are often described as "stress junkies." In the next section, which discusses types of workaholics, you will find a category of workaholic I call the high-stimulus-seeking workaholic, who matches the description of a type A personality.

The most common problems experienced by workaholics include increased levels of job stress and burnout, work-family conflicts, problems with coworkers, health problems, low levels of life satisfaction, and a lack of enjoyment of leisure time and activities apart from work.

TYPES OF WORKAHOLICS

Robinson (2000) suggests several types of workaholics (types 1–4), as follows.

Type 1: The Relentless Workaholic   Relentless workaholics work all the time. They believe that work is more important than relationships or anything else in life. According to Robinson, they are perfectionists who demand perfectionism in others, have many projects going at once, and are admired for their hard work and competence by others outside of their families.

Type 2: The Procrastinating Workaholic   The second category is the procrastinating workaholic, who waits until the last possible minute, goes into a panic, and then works frantically to finish a task. Unlike relentless workaholics, whose productivity is usually quite high, procrastinating workaholics go through long periods during which they do not work. Robinson believes that the reason these workaholics go through long periods of nonactivity is that they are so preoccupied with perfection that they cannot start a project.

An Example. I have a number of students who are procrastinating workaholics. They usually come to me with excuses about their work, which they've completed just before the assignment is due even though they've known the due date months in advance. Their work is usually poor, with many mistakes. Their usual excuse is a computer problem, an illness, or a family problem. When asked why they've waited until the last minute, they can't provide a legitimate excuse. If you have them in enough classes, you know that their behavior continues on in the new class. Whether waiting until the last minute to complete an assignment is caused by perfectionistic tendencies, laziness, or disorganization is hard to determine, but they put themselves at risk on the job and are not well thought of in most organizations.

Type 3: The High-Stimulus-Seeking Workaholic   A third type of workaholic is the workaholic who is easily bored and constantly seeks stimulation and excitement. Robinson (2000) believes that some seek excitement in a relatively safe way by "creating tight work deadlines, keeping many projects going at one time, taking on big challenges at work, and having the chronic inability to relax without intense stimulation. Others live on the edge and engage in high-risk jobs or activities, such as playing the stock market, parachute jumping, or working triage in a hospital emergency room" (p. 43). High-stimulus-seeking workaholics are easily bored with detail, have difficulty following through, and get their satisfaction by creating new projects.

Type 4: The Bureaupathic Workaholic   Bureaupathic workaholics are the people with whom we hate to be on committees. There isn't a rule, policy, standard, or ploy they won't use to control projects, committee meetings, or work assignments. Their primary function is to set up roadblocks to the completion of projects. They think they bring order and rationality to the process, but what they really bring is chaos, disruption, and easy projects made impossible. The term *bureaupathic* is used to imply the worst qualities of top-down organizations: that they are slow to change; illogical in the way decisions are made; primarily concerned with the quality of life of those who work in the organization and not with customers and clients, and are endlessly rule- and policy-driven, with little sense of the need to change even when the organization is in deep trouble.

Bureaupathic workaholics prolong assignments and create additional work. Others may be ready to move on, but these workaholics hold everything up by overanalyzing, tearing ideas apart, and getting bogged down in minute detail. They drive everyone a little crazy.

An Example. A friend gave me a good example of this type of workaholic. Her husband and a neighbor were playing tennis on the courts owned by their home owner's association (HOA). In the middle of a set, the president of the HOA, who had known them both for more than 15 years and knew they lived in the HOA condos, ran out onto the court and demanded that they show proof that they were entitled to play on the courts. He caused a real scene. When the next HOA meeting was held, he showed evidence in the by-laws that he was supposed to check periodically on the people using the tennis courts to ensure that they had a legitimate reason to be there. He was completely unable to see that he knew that the people playing on the court were members of the HOA and argued that he was just "going by the book" and doing his job. He was, of course, removed from his position because it was clear that although they needed someone who was responsible to be president of the HOA, the prior president lacked people skills, good judgment, and common sense. Unfortunately, too many people in similar positions are controlling to a point of creating deep resentment.

I would also suggest some additional types of workaholics (types 5–10).

Type 5: The Loner Workaholic   Type 5 is the withdrawn workaholic who prefers to work alone. They work hard and want to be needed and approved of, but they do not want to be controlled or dominated. This type of workaholic prefers to keep their emotional distance from others and to be left alone to do their work.

An Example. In many ways, I'm a loner workaholic. I've worked successfully in organizations and have been dean of a school of social work and the executive director of a family service agency. All my jobs have required that I work cooperatively with others, and yet I prefer to work alone. I have friends and family relationships that are sustaining and give me great pleasure, but when it comes to my writing projects and teaching responsibilities, I enjoy doing them in the early morning when the sun is coming up over the lush high-mountain scenery of my home in the Arizona mountains. The deer, hawks, eagles, bobcats, javelina, and other creatures that come to my office door in the early morning to visit give me joy I can't quite express.

I know I wouldn't get the same pleasure out of working in a group. I want to get right in there and do the job. Too much talking or thinking messes things up for me . I work early in the morning (from 6 to 10 o'clock), break for tennis and coffee, and come back in mid-afternoon to work several more hours. It's a very satisfying schedule of about six hours of work most days. If you know anything about writing, that's a pretty productive schedule. I love the e-mail exchanges with my students and the actual teaching, but developing my courses and writing my books are done best when I'm alone. I'm pretty certain about what I do, so feedback isn't what I'm looking for, unless I ask for it. I like working with people who understand my preference for working alone, but when I contact them, I want them to be as compulsive in responding as I am. I know I'm not a loner because I have lots of people in my life; I don't think I'm a workaholic because I have so many other interests, but call it what you like—I get great pleasure out of working alone. Because I work very efficiently, I have that much more time to devote to the other things in life that I enjoy: my family, tennis, hiking, reading mystery books, watching films, corresponding with friends, and traveling.

Type 6: The Frightened Workaholic   This type of workaholic is afraid of losing their job, and rather than having clear guidelines that help them understand the expectations of the job, they catastrophizes the job's demands into impossible-to-achieve work expectations that take all of their time, and more, to achieve. Though they work very hard, a good deal of their work is ordinary in quality. It just takes this type of workaholic much longer to do the job because much of their energy is spent on anxious and unrealistic thinking about the job.

Type 7: The Burned-Out Workaholic   This type of workaholic is so burned out they can hardly muster the energy to do the job, but out of a lack of other interests and activities or a dismal or nonexistent personal life, they keep working hard at a job that gives them no satisfaction and which they may actually dislike to the extent of becoming physically ill while they work. Without help, these people burn up and often develop depression and anxiety-related problems that make work exceedingly difficult.

Type 8: The Incompetent Workaholic   We like to think of workaholics as hardworking and superproductive, but some workaholics have to work that much harder because, truth be known, they just don't have the ability to do the job. We've all known workaholics like this. They never take lunch breaks, stay late, come in over the weekend, but never seem to get much done. Rather than looking for psychological reasons for their work addiction, it might be better to think of them as lacking competence. Moving into a less demanding job would probably eliminate their work addiction.

Type 9: The Dictatorial Workaholic   This type of workaholic gets sadistic pleasure out of working others to death. He uses insults and threats to get others to work as hard as he does, if not harder. He uses intimidation and put-downs to eliminate rewards and never gives positive feedback. While he thrives on the pain he inflicts on others, including his family, he benefits from the hard work he requires of others. Because he never gives others credit for their achievements and coops their achievements by making them his own, he always looks to outsiders as the most capable person around. This type of workaholic often rises to the top of organizations. It comes as a surprise to others not familiar with how the dictatorial workaholic functions that they create such unhappiness and often are so disliked by others in an organization.

Type 10: The Manic-Depressive Workaholic   Occasionally, we find people who achieve at a very high level because they have manic episodes that last long enough for them to get incredible amounts of work done. During manic highs, they may work for days without sleep before succumbing to the inevitable low they experience as the chemical nature of their condition shifts to depression. Some people have manic highs all the time. What distinguishes them from other types of workaholics is that there is often something very troubling about their behavior and the work they produce. They appear to be high on drugs (and sometimes they are). I've read work written by students and employees during manic phases that is often just gibberish. This type of workaholic may function well for a time but often the manic episodes become troublesome to coworkers and often lead to obvious mistakes that outweigh the quantity of work completed.

Personal Story: A Hardworking Physician
Finds Happiness in Retirement

"I retired in 2001 at age 61 as an academic pathologist from the University of Nebraska. Was I working more than I wanted to? Perhaps. Mainly, I saw time slipping by and wanted to do other things. I also felt that I had done all I could at the university, and it was starting to become less interesting for me.

"There were many things that I wanted to do with my life, including my passion for woodworking. I've continued to be involved in a number of activities related to my work as a pathologist. My teaching activities continue, including lecture and small group, but fewer in number. A colleague asked me to write a chapter for a medical textbook, which I did gladly. In anticipation of being asked to do the chapter again, I have kept up on the subject of my chapter with appropriate references.

"In 2004, I was hired by the state of Nebraska to do administrative work in the area of behavioral health reform. I spent eight months traveling the state to assess the progress of the process. It was a most rewarding time for me.

"In 2005, my wife and I were asked to go to Kabul, Afghanistan, to do faculty development in teaching methods at Kabul Medical University. We were asked to return again a few months later to repeat our program for other faculty. I returned to Kabul Medical in 2007 to give an update to an international conference on Afghan medical education. In addition, we have brought Kabul Medical faculty to our medical school in Nebraska for further instruction for an extended period of time. I did a fair amount of work with those faculty.

"As a Civil War buff, I have continued to go to various seminars and tours of Civil War battlefields. My library has a large collection of Civil War books. The Second World War also interests me. Two years ago, my son and I visited Bayeaux in Normandy and walked Omaha Beach. Again, I have a good library of World War II literature.

"Woodworking has been a lifelong enjoyment for me. Now I like to build and give away furniture. Another lifelong hobby is amateur radio. My call is KØEMC. I love Morse code and talking to folks from all around our country and the world.

"I am active in organized medicine, both at the local and state levels. Both local and state boards of directors occupy some of my time. I am also president of our local medical foundation that donates funds to local nonprofit organizations.

"Teaching became my great love as I went through my academic career, and I still enjoy it today, but now I don't have the other duties. I do what I really love to do. Furthermore, I am also on the admissions committee for the medical school, something I'd always wanted to do. It is time consuming but fun for me.

"I am also involved in my church, serving on the council and assisting in liturgical duties on Sunday.

"As you can see, I do very much like to work, but now I get to do exactly what I want. When evening comes, I get tired very quickly because of my activity. Additionally, I walk for one hour each day to keep up my physical stamina. Life is very good in retirement, and though I keep very busy, I have the time to do all the things I've always wanted to do, including spending time with my family, woodworking, traveling, and continuing my work in medicine and teaching. Life is very good."—James Newland, MD, Emeritus Professor of Pathology and Microbiology, University of Nebraska Medical Center

SUMMARY

This chapter discussed the various types of workaholics and gave examples of how workaholic behavior can interfere with relationships and cause problems on the job. Many of the types of workaholics are probably familiar to the reader, but the workaholic who controls others by using the rules and policies of the organization to enhance his or her status is a workaholic we all seem to know and often find difficult to work with. The chapter ended with a personal story from a physician who has found in retirement the time to do a number of new and exciting things as well as many old loves he hadn't had the time to complete while he worked.

REFERENCES

Douglas, E.J., & Morris, R.L. (2006). Workaholic, or just hard worker? *Career Development International, 11*, 394–417.

Friedman, M., & Rosenman, R.H. (1974). *Type A behavior and your heart.* New York: Knopf.

Griffiths, M. (2005). Workaholism is still a useful construct. *Addiction Research and Theory, 13*, 97–100.

Machlowitz, M. (1980). *Workaholics.* New York: Mentor.

Robinson, B.E. (2000). A typology of workaholics with implications for counselors. *Journal of Addictions and Offender Counseling, 21*, 34–49.

CHAPTER 3

The Physical and Emotional Impact of Work Addiction

A number of researchers have found a relationship between work addiction and physical and emotional health problems as well as marital discord and divorce, and problems developed by children as a result of a parent's work addiction. Although it may seem obvious that people who work a great deal and are under significant amounts of stress develop physical and emotional problems, the research is contradictory. Some workaholics develop health problems, but not all of them do. However, symptoms of serious health problems or emotional problems tied to overwork are indications that something needs to be done to reduce the stress of work, a subject I will discuss more in future chapters.

HEALTH PROBLEMS

According to Stein (2009), constant overwork "creates huge surges of adrenaline, which floods the body and taxes every physical function, especially that of the heart. The adrenaline can contribute to high blood-pressure and to the buildup of plaque in heart vessels, increasing the risk of heart attacks and strokes" (p. 1). She also notes that workaholics suffer from a number of stress disorders, including anxiety attacks, ulcers, and burnout, as well as "depression that can lead to suicide" (p. 1). Because workaholics have addictive personalities and are often in denial about the impact their work addictions have on their physical and mental health, workaholics often give the illusion of being in excellent health and having a great deal of energy, when their denial of fatigue often leads to workaholics being "taken out by a heart attack or stroke, or a collapse with a really cata-strophic illness" (p. 1).

A number of research studies have found a link between type A personal-ities, their tendency to work too hard, and heart problems (Booth-Kewley & Friedman, 1987). Scott (2007) reports that type A personalities experience an 84 percent higher risk of high blood pressure and are virtually certain to have heart disease by age 65. Job stress, common to type A personalities, often leads to metabolic syndrome (weight problems, high cholesterol, and adult-onset diabetes), which is a common precondition for heart attack and stroke.

Spence and Robbins (1992) report that people with high degrees of workaholism have more health complaints and higher stress levels than nonworkaholics. Burke (2000) found that workaholics have more psycho-somatic symptoms as well as greater concerns about physical and psy-chological well-being than nonworkaholics. Burke and Matthiesen (2004) found that workaholics often suffer from depression and exhaustion. In discussing the similarities between alcoholism and workaholism, Robin-son (2000) found that workaholism "can lead to unmanageable life, family disintegration, serious health problems, and even death" (p. 34). Burke, Matthiesen, and Pallesen (2006) found that workaholism is often related to burnout, which, if untreated, often cycles into depression. In Japan, there is a syndrome known as *karoshi* or "death by overwork," a problem that should give us all pause as we look at health and work addiction.

Though it makes sense that people who work too hard will often suffer from health problems, it's important to remember that not all workaholics are the same. In chapter 2, I noted the different types of workaholics. Not all suffer from stress-related health problems.

THE IMPACT OF WORK ADDICTION ON RELATIONSHIPS AND FAMILY LIFE

The negative impact of workaholism on families and relationships has been written about at length. Oates (1971) observed that workaholics are socially inadequate in their home lives and have difficulties with personal relationships. Robinson (1989) suggested that excessive work often pre-vents workaholics from forming and maintaining intimate relationships. Killinger (1991) found that workaholics have limited intimacy with spouses and use work as a substitute for all other relationships. Other researchers have found that workaholism results in much higher divorce rates (Klaft & Kleiner, 1988), less frequent sexual intercourse (Pietropinto, 1986), and a lack of sensitivity to the feelings of others (Engstrom & Juroe, 1979). Jack-son (1992) found that workaholics tend to be far more irritable at work and in their personal lives than those who are not work addicted.

Robinson and Flowers (2002) found that workaholism is related to greater marital dissatisfaction because spouses often feel ignored, neglected, and unappreciated and believe they are carrying the emotional burdens of the marriage and parenting. Spouses also feel that they cannot measure up to their spouses and often feel guilty for wanting more from their marriages when their spouses work so hard. The researchers found that marriages with work-addicted spouses have a much higher divorce rate (55%) than marriages without a work-addicted spouse (16%).

In terms of the effect of the workaholism of parents on children, Oates (1971) found that children saw their parents as preoccupied with work, always in a rush to get somewhere, often irritable and lacking a sense of humor, and depressed about their work. Robinson (1998) reported that many adult children of workaholics suffer greater depression, higher anxiety, and greater obsessive-compulsive tendencies than adult children of nonworkaholics. A study comparing adult children of workaholics with adult children of alcoholics (Carroll & Robinson, 2000) indicated that adult children of workaholics had higher scores in depression than adults from alcoholic homes and adults from nonworkaholic homes.

To be fair, O'Driscoll and Brady (2004) found that although the research tended to suggest that workaholics have problems in their personal lives, the author's research failed to find a great deal of difference between the personal lives of workaholics and those of nonworkaholics. The authors point out that it is difficult to differentiate between people who are work addicted and those who just work hard because many of us work very hard. Furthermore, the term *workaholic* is often vague and may not be used correctly. My observations of retired people who exhibit workaholic characteristics suggests that many of them, when asked, have satisfying personal relationships, but when spouses and children are asked, they often talk about the negative side of trying to maintain a relationship with someone who puts all of their energy into work and how little is left over for them. Because there are certainly benefits of work addiction, including affluence and status, many spouses and children put up with work addiction because there is so much to gain from the labor of the workaholic spouse and parent.

WHY PEOPLE DEVELOP WORK ADDICTIONS

Many people in the mental health field believe that work addictions are the result of problems encountered early in life. Let's consider what some of these problems might be and how people react to them.

1. Probably the most common reason why a person may become work addicted is that he grew up in a family with severe financial problems. Children who grow up in poverty often feel deeply insecure and develop work habits that try to ensure stability and security in their lives. For these people, working hard, even working more than hard, can be justified as a way of staying safe. Many people who grow up in poverty are classic overachievers who work

very hard in school and later in jobs. For them, the insecurity of poverty helps reinforce work habits that may, over time, but not necessarily, become compulsive and workaholic.

2. Children who grow up in homes where there are deep insecurities often respond to those insecurities through very hard work. Children who have been abused or neglected or whose parents have died or abandoned them recognize early in life that the only way they will survive is to depend on themselves. Many of these children are resilient and overcompensate for the social and emotional traumas they've experienced in their lives by doing well in school and then doing well at work. However, serious problems early in life often affect their development, and many resilient children develop early depression and anxiety problems even as they do well in school. They are hard workers early in life, and as their insecurities deepen as they mature, they often use the only mechanism they have for dealing with problems: very hard work.

3. Children who grow up in families that have very high standards for achievement sometimes become perfectionistic adults who are prone to workaholism because of a need to do things more perfectly than anyone could ever hope for. Perfectionism is one of the primary characteristics of workaholics.

4. Demanding jobs and professions in which not achieving can result in the loss of a career can certainly make people workaholics. Lawyers who need to bill many hours a week, physicians who see 30 or more patients a day, and teachers who have to teach ever larger classrooms with more and more work are examples of people in jobs in which not being able to maintain a high level of work output places your job and career in jeopardy.

5. Certain occupations that require long hours, such as medicine and law, not only result in work addiction, but many times the work addiction leads to burnout and early termination of careers. These highly stressful fields of work are often structured to expect people to work 80 hours a week and more and are certainly high on the list of occupations in which people become work addicted and are likely to burn out. Davis (2000) found that physician insurers have seen disability claims from doctors climb by more than 60 percent since 1990. Eighty-five percent of physicians say their family lives often or sometimes suffer from the demands of their profession, and 30 percent say that they would change their profession today if they could.

6. Some children have been taught or are forced to take care of parents and siblings because of parental illness, parental substance abuse, parental mental health problems or by single parents who work and give the responsibility of caring for the home to the child who shows the greatest ability to deal with the added stress. These caretakers often assume great responsibility in organizations and see their role as one of making certain that the organization functions well, even if this isn't part of their job description. They feel compelled to make sure everyone is doing well. They are often overworked; develop problems with anxiety; and though told that they are indispensable, often fail to get the rewards and promotions other workers are given. As they slowly begin to realize that they are working far too hard but receive little praise and few rewards, they often tend to experience burn-out and depression. They are workaholics because overwork replays the feelings of

pride they received in their role as caretaker when they were children. Those early life scripts that children develop have a way of continuing on in adulthood.

A MEASURE OF WORK ADDICTION: THE OLDER ADULT WORK ADDICTION SCALE

Now that you know a bit about work addiction, it might be helpful for you to determine your level of work addiction. Please answer the following questions by rating yourself on the Older Adult Work Addiction Scale (OAWAS) using the rating scale of 1 (*never true*), 2 (*sometimes true*), 3 (*often true*), or 4 (*always true*). Put the number that best describes your current work habits on the blank line at the beginning of each statement. The first answer that comes to mind is usually the most honest and accurate one. After you have responded to all 25 statements, add up the numbers you have written on the blank lines to get your total score. The OAWAS was developed by the author (Glicken, 2009).

1. _____ As I've gotten older, I've become more work addicted than when I was younger.
2. _____ People have always been jealous of my work ethic.
3. _____ I have a strong desire to do things right.
4. _____ I'm very competitive in most things in life.
5. _____ The more money you make, the harder you've worked.
6. _____ I don't know how to use leisure time and work to occupy myself.
7. _____ Once I start a task, it's difficult for me not to finish.
8. _____ I wake up at night thinking about work.
9. _____ I think about work during social events and parties.
10. _____ My family often tells me that I work too hard.
11. _____ I only see a doctor when I'm really sick.
12. _____ I have been told by my doctor to lose weight but can't seem to do it.
13. _____ I feel jittery when I have nothing to do.
14. _____ I think about upsetting things that happened at work even though they happened long ago.
15. _____ I get very impatient when I have to wait for most things (a table at a restaurant, a doctor's appointment, etc.).
16. _____ It's difficult for me to talk to others about work.
17. _____ I've been putting off retirement because I'm worried that I won't know what to do with myself.
18. _____ Most of my work life has been spent working hard at jobs I didn't particularly like.
19. _____ People think that I'm pushy and demanding.

20. ____ My relationships with my family have been negatively affected by my work.

21. ____ I drink alcohol or use drugs to cope with stress or loneliness.

22. ____ I don't like to delegate work to others because they seldom get it done right.

23. ____ I worry a lot.

24. ____ I feel down when I'm not busy.

25. ____ It's hard for me to accept help from others.

What the Results Mean   Those of you scoring in the upper fourth (75–100) are considered highly workaholic. If you scored in this range, it could mean that you are on your way to burnout, and new research suggests that family members may be experiencing emotional repercussions as well. Those scoring in the middle range (50–74) are considered mildly workaholic. If you scored in this range, there is hope. With acceptance and modifications, you and your loved ones can prevent negative lasting effects. Those scoring in the lowest range (25–49) are not considered workaholic. If you scored in this range, you are probably a hard worker instead of a workaholic. You needn't worry that your work style will negatively affect yourself or others.

How Did I Do?   My score was 64, or about the middle of the mildly work-addicted range. I think a more accurate way of describing me would be to use the Douglas and Morris (2006) term of *low-leisure hard worker*. It's true that I don't handle leisure time well, and work becomes a way of occupying my time when there isn't anything else that I want to do. This isn't to say that I don't do leisure things, because I do, but when they don't excite me, I tend to work, but it's usually enjoyable work like writing books and teaching.

As I wrote this section of the book, I thought I was done writing for the day. It was Sunday morning, and I was getting ready to go to the local Unity church service. Just as I was getting ready to leave, I had an idea for the book and wanted to capture it in print or risked losing it. I wrote for five minutes, made church on time, and returned home after church to polish the work I'd done. I look at writing books as fun, not as hard work or a work addiction, but that's my read on it.

I'm not pleased with my score of 64 because I think I've mellowed out a bit as I've aged, but at 69, I'd like to see myself move increasingly toward being a hard worker rather than a workaholic. I've worked hard all my life. I think I can slack off a bit now and do many of the things I've always wanted to do: scuba dive at the Great Barrier Reef; learn to tango at a tango bar in Buenos Aires; write a publishable mystery; teach my grandchildren about nature; and many other things that still burn inside me. How about you? How do you interpret the results, and how do they affect your sense of your work addiction? Are the results a surprise, or do they seem to be consistent with how you view yourself? And more important, how do you think being a workaholic will affect you after you retire? That's what I'm going to write about in the next few chapters.

SUMMARY

This chapter discussed the physical and emotional impacts of workaholic behavior and concluded that the toll of work addiction can be very serious. To help better determine your level of work addiction, an instrument I created was included in the chapter, along with a scoring guide, to help you determine your level of work addiction.

REFERENCES

Booth-Kewley, S., & Friedman, H.S. (1987). Psychological predictors of heart disease: A quantitative review. *Psychological Bulletin, 101*, 343–362.

Burke, R.J. (2000). Workaholism in organizations: Psychological and physical well-being consequences. *Stress Medicine, 16*, 11–16.

Burke, R.J., & Matthiesen, S. (2004). Short communication: Workaholism among Norwegian journalists—antecedents and consequences. *Stress and Health: Journal of the International Society for the Investigation of Stress, 20*, 301–308.

Burke, R.J., Matthiesen, S.B., & Pallesen, S. (2006). Workaholism, organizational life and well-being of Norwegian nursing staff. *Career Development International, 11*, 463–468.

Carroll, J.J., & Robinson, B.E. (2000). Depression and parentification among adults as related to paternal workaholism and alcoholism. *The Family Journal, 8*, 33–41.

Davis, K.G. (2000). *The personality traits that make you a good doctor may also make you a target for burnout.* Retrieved July 12, 2009, from http://www.aafp.org/fpm/20000400/70prev.html.

Douglas, E.J., & Morris, R.L. (2006). Workaholic, or just hard worker? *Career Development International, 11*, 394–417.

Engstrom, T.W., & Juroe, D.J. (1979). *The work trap.* Old Tappan, NJ: Fleming H. Revell.

Flowers, C.P., & Robinson, B. (2002). A structural and discriminant analysis of the work addiction risk test. *Educational and Psychological Measurement, 62*, 517–526.

Jackson, D.L. (1992). *Correlates of physical and emotional health among male and female workaholics.* Unpublished doctoral dissertation, University of Oregon, Portland.

Killinger, B. (1991). *Workaholics: The respectable addicts.* Sydney, Australia: Simon & Schuster.

Klaft, R.P., & Kleiner, B.H. (1988). Understanding workaholics. *Business, 38*(3), 37–40.

Oates, W.E. (1971). *Confessions of a workaholic: The facts about work addiction.* New York: World Publishing.

O'Driscoll, P., & Brady, E.C. (2004). The impact of workaholism on personal relationships. *British Journal of Guidance and Counselling, 32*, 171–186.

Pietropinto, A. (1986, May). The workaholic spouse: A survey analysis. *Medical Aspects of Human Sexuality*, 94–98.

Robinson, B.E. (1989). *Work addiction: Hidden legacies of adult children.* Deerfield Beach, FL: Health Communications.

Robinson, B.E. (1998). *Chained to the desk: A guidebook for workaholics, the partners and children, and the clinicians who treat them.* New York: New York University Press.

Robinson, B.E. (2000). A typology of workaholics with implications for counselors. *Journal of Addictions and Offender Counseling, 21*, 34–49.

Scott, E.S. (2007). *Type A personality traits: Characteristics and effects of a type A personality.* Retrieved August 6, 2009, from http://stress.about.com/od/understandingstress/a/type_a_person.htm.

Spence, J.T., & Robbins, A.S. (1992). Workaholism: Definition, measurement, and preliminary results. *Journal of Personality Assessment, 58*, 160–178.

Stein, L. (2009). *Workaholism: It's no longer seen as a respectable vice, but as a serious problem that can have life-threatening consequences.* Retrieved August 2, 2009, from http://www.ahealthyme.com/topic/workaholism.

CHAPTER 4

The 10 Irrational Ideas That Get Workaholics into Emotional Difficulty

We often base important life decisions on irrational ideas, or ideas that seem logical on the face of it but, when the consequences are looked at, often cause considerable problems as we age. These ideas form a way of looking at the world and directing our behavior to support the ideas that we've developed over time. Sometimes these ideas or perceptions lead to great success, but often they end up creating a host of problems. Such is the case with work addiction. The following 10 irrational ideas are those that are particularly likely to result in serious physical and emotional problems.

1. *Work is the most important thing in my life.* It's true that some people believe that their work trumps everything else, but when it's more important than our health, our families, and the pleasures we might get out of life, it's an obsession. Work is important as a source of financial security, and some people get incredible satisfaction from their work, but at some point in time, it's important to enjoy the other pleasures in life. As you get older and are not as able to put your all into work, if you have no outside interests, what fills the gap? Making work the most important aspect of your life tends to push people away, inhibits real intimacy with others, and makes children and family secondary. When work is no longer available, it leaves you with nothing to take its place.

2. *I won't succeed unless I work harder than anyone else around me.* That's possible, but how do you measure working harder than anyone else? Some people don't need to work as hard because they work smart. Others are naturals at the job or have more ability. Working harder doesn't necessarily mean that you'll be successful. The better idea is that you learn the job and work smart and hard but not to the extent that you think working harder (i.e., putting

in more hours than anyone else) will actually lead to more success. In fact, working harder than anyone else raises the possibility that you will be seen as incompetent if you don't produce in keeping with the number of hours worked.

3. *If I don't succeed, I'll be a failure.* Only you make the judgment that you're a failure. What others think should be of no consequence in the way you define yourself. If it is, you'll constantly be trying to please people, and you'll always find someone you can't please no matter how much you try. It's far better if you try to please yourself. I've been able to keep writing successful books by never caring what others think of my work. Of course, I'd like readers to learn from my books in ways that are beneficial to their lives. But most people aren't geared to giving praise. My positive feelings about myself and my work come from getting up early in the morning and only having a minimal idea of what I'm going to write about. I sit at the computer and get to work, and amazingly, I often come up with work that makes me feel happy, even giddy. It's not what others say about me that matters; rather, it's whether I can meet my own standards for the work I do. I often forget what I've written in prior books because once a book is done, rather than dwelling on it, I want to move to a new project that will help me learn about new topics I know nothing about. My positive feelings come from the process of writing, not from what others say about me. In that sense, I'm an inner-directed person. I get my good feelings about myself by setting and working toward my own goals. Outer-directed people get their good feelings from what others say and think about them. These people are always trying to please others so that they are well thought of. Inner-directed people couldn't care less about what others think.

Another way of looking at this is through what psychologists call *locus of control*, or our personal philosophies of life. People with an internal locus of control believe that they control their destinies. They think hard work and competence will lead to success. People with an external locus of control believe that our life outcomes are determined by luck, chance, and fate. There's not much we can do to determine our success in life because it's up to others.

In a number of research studies, people with an internal locus of control were shown to be healthier emotionally and physically than those with an external locus of control. They understand that they are in control of their lives and that the way to succeed isn't a mystery or something controlled by others. We have control over the careers we choose, the amount of work we put into those careers, how we view family and loved ones, and what we do with our personal lives. People who have an external locus of control are much more likely to become workaholics. Anyone who sees the world realistically knows that work addiction will exclude many of the things in life that sustain us and keep us healthy.

4. *Unless I work very hard, everything at work will fall apart.* This irrational idea is what psychologists call *catastrophizing*, or the idea that unless we can control everything in life by working hard and being eternally vigilant, our lives will fall apart. People who try to control everything are often prone to anxiety problems or have what we've come to call obsessive-compulsive disorder (OCD). This is a problem in which people try to control life events by compulsively doing things ritualistically over and over in an attempt to make certain

that everything will go well. Workaholics are often thought of as obsessive-compulsive people because the hard work they do on jobs becomes a compulsive activity and is repeated again and again to make certain everything will be OK. For many people with OCD, the work required to keep anything bad from happening often leads to more time spent in repetitive behavior than in actual work.

5. *If I can't do it the right way, there's no point in doing it at all.* This is the perfectionist's motto, but in reality we do many things each day that we don't do well. If we were perfectionists, than the simple things that give us pleasure but we don't always do well (e.g., playing sports, cooking, and gardening) we wouldn't do at all. Where would that leave us? The fact is that whatever we do, there's always someone who does it as well or better than us. Demanding perfection in everything we do is a recipe for unhappiness.

When I began writing professional articles in my mid-20s but worried that I'd never get an article done well enough to get anything published, a wise person told me that my job was to do the writing in the best way I knew how. The editor's job was to decide if it was good enough to publish. There was nothing I could do to control whether it was published other than to keep sending it on to other journals until it either got published or no one wanted to publish it. In that event, I'd learned something, and maybe with some revisions I'd get the work in a good enough state to publish. It took a while, but someone published what I'd written, and since then, I've had no trouble publishing articles or books.

Could my books be better if I took more time to write them? Maybe, but I take the time I'm given by the editor, and after that, if she wants revisions or corrections to make it better, that's her decision. By taking an antiperfectionistic approach to writing, this is my 14th book. I'm proud of all of them, but other than wanting my books to be very good, I never have thoughts of making them perfect. Why? Because I'd still be working on my first book if that were the case. Do I cringe when I see things in my books I could have written better? Sometimes I do, but by then I'm well on my way to writing another book or working on another project, and that's what I'm focused on. I began working on my first book in 2000. Each book has been easier to write because writing, like many other skills, takes time and practice. I also know that my books are professionally edited and that many of the mistakes I've made will be corrected. I read my books very carefully in the editing stage, but even then, mistakes are made. If I were to dwell on them, I would never write another book.

6. *I'll only be successful in my personal life if I'm successful at work.* Sorry, but the reality is that though most people might like us, for reasons we can't explain, some people won't. Trying to be liked is one of those no-win approaches to life that gets many people into difficulty. While we hope that we can get along with everyone and have good working relationships, we can't expect everyone to like us. Furthermore, what happens at work doesn't influence what happens in our personal lives. Being successful at work has no impact on whether people outside of work like or admire us. You learn that very early on as a teacher. You can be the most successful teacher the world has ever known, but someone in the class isn't buying it, and for reasons you can't explain, he or she doesn't see you as a successful teacher and doesn't like you.

I've read hundreds of evaluations of my teaching, and even though they're usually good, inevitably, someone doesn't think so. My success as a writer and any past success I've had as a teacher and mental health professional is meaningless. Can you imagine everyone caring deeply about you in retirement because you were a success at work? I play tennis with former CEOs of large corporations. Some are nice; others aren't. What they did in their work life has no bearing on whether I like them.

7. *Work is the only way I have of dealing with the demons that haunt my life.* Better to get some good help to rid yourself of demons from the past than to work yourself to death trying to get rid of them. Many workaholics use work to deal with feelings of insecurity and lack of self-esteem, but the workplace is only part of your life. When you go home at night, the demons are still there. Work has done nothing to drive them away. Later in the book, I'll discuss dealing with strong feelings of insecurity and low self-esteem, but all the success in the world can't make you feel good about yourself when over the years you've had a negative sense of yourself and your worthiness as a person.

8. *If I don't continue working very hard, I'll become bored, depressed, and anxious.* In fact, you might, but the time to start dealing with fears about the future is now. Don't make this a self-fulfilling prophecy so that you believe something is going to happen in the future and therefore it does. What's irrational about this idea is that nothing is inevitable. If you feel that way, then surely you'll experience all of the unhappiness you've been predicting for yourself. Inner-directed people do the work necessary to change their behavior so that they can deal with the future. Outer-directed people let things happen to them. In a study of working-class retirees I discuss in more detail in a later chapter, men who assumed that life was over after they retired were much more prone to health problems and depression. They did nothing to broaden themselves but rather continued past behavior such as drinking with the guys or playing poker. Most lived very lonely lives. Those men who retired and became involved in volunteer work and thought of retirement as a time to improve themselves through education and reading were far healthier and more satisfied with life.

9. *It's not what you know, it's who you know.* Of course, this is sometimes true, but for most of us, it isn't. Even if we have special relationships with people who can make things happen for us, we don't always want to ask favors for fear of alienating them. Giving people that much power over us is also a mistake because we assume they can and will do us favors if we ask, when often they won't. And finally, most of us know that calling in a favor means we'll owe someone, and paying that person back can sometimes be costly. It's not who we know, it's what we know and how we use it that impresses people and gets us the rewards we desire. Knowing the reward you desire is also very important.

10. *It'll never get done correctly unless I do it myself.* This is one of the cardinal rules followed by most workaholics. It's irrational because there are many things we're not good at and other people are. Not using the expertise of others means that you might do the job more poorly than they would. It's also irrational because in any job, doing everything means that you've loaded yourself down with heaps of work because you don't trust people to do their

jobs. Not being able to delegate is inconsistent with the way most organizations operate and tends to offend people. Furthermore, it's an indication that you think so little of your coworkers that you dismiss their capabilities—this is not a good way to be in most organizations.

A PRIMER ON HOW TO DEAL WITH IRRATIONAL THINKING

Just as we are capable of telling ourselves whatever we want to justify our thinking about a subject, we can also learn to tell ourselves that our thinking and perceptions may be flawed, and if we look at issues in a logical way, many of the thoughts that produce problems in our lives can be changed for the better.

To understand this notion, let's pretend that we're on the 18th floor of a building with only one entrance. A cute little poodle comes through the door. Most of us will be amused and will even want the poodle to come to us. We perceive no danger at all, and we think of a dog coming into the room as unusual but certainly not dangerous. Replace the poodle with a 125-pound Doberman pinscher foaming at the mouth and growling. There's no way out of the room because the dog is blocking the only entrance. We would immediately perceive the situation as dangerous and worry about how we might get out of the room without the dog harming us. You see, we think before we act, and our thinking is translated into sentences we silently tell ourselves—what have been called *self-sentences*.

Most of our thinking is pretty logical, but to this list of 10 irrational ideas that get us into trouble on the job we could probably add hundreds more. It's these irrational thoughts, ideas, and perceptions that get us into emotional difficulty. If we can change our irrational thinking, we can often prevent ourselves from becoming unhappy. Let me show you a simple way to undo irrational ideas. Let's use a simple *A-B-C-D-E* formula, as in the following:

A. *Something happens to you.* Your boss doesn't greet you in the morning as you pass each other in the hall.

B. *You have an irrational perception.* You immediately think that your boss's oversight signifies something awful. Maybe you'll be downsized, or maybe you've done something to make your boss dislike you. It's really important that your boss likes you. In fact, it's very important that *everyone* likes you. If someone doesn't like you, you feel insecure.

C. *You become very anxious.* Your perception of the experience with your boss causes you to vow to work harder so that your boss will like you more and nothing bad will happen to you. In other words, without knowing why your boss ignored you, you've talked yourself into workaholic behavior.

D. *Resolution.* Instead of becoming anxious and overworking yourself, you go to the source, your boss, and ask if everything is OK. You explain that he seemed very unhappy when you met, and you let him explain that it had nothing to do with you; rather, his daughter had just run off with the worst possible guy, and she's going to ruin her life (now he's becoming irrational because he doesn't know his presumption to be a fact).

E. *Happiness*. You now know your boss isn't unhappy with you, and you can feel fairly certain that your work is acceptable and that you don't have to become a workaholic. See how easy it is?

Irrational ideas are often part of our culture, but for many of us, they have been drummed into us by parents and other important people in our lives (teachers, bosses, spouses, loved ones, and friends). It takes a certain amount of practice to overcome irrational thinking and the problematic self-talking we do that creates problems in our lives. I worked with children as a school social worker when I was just out of graduate school. They were wonderful at learning to identify irrational thinking and doing something about it. If an eight-year-old can do it, so can you. I promise that as you learn to recognize irrational thoughts, beliefs, and perceptions and counter them with rational thinking, you'll be less anxious, angry, or depressed.

SUMMARY

This chapter discussed irrational ideas that are often used by workaholics to justify their work addictions. Just as you can use irrational ideas and perceptions to justify behavior that becomes problematic, you can counter irrational ideas by understanding the self-sentences you use that get you into emotional difficulty. A short explanation of how to do this was provided. In further chapters understanding the way counselors help workaholics with seriously intrusive problems will be discussed.

PART II

Preretirement Planning

Before retiring, most successfully retired people begin to think carefully about retirement. Chapter 5 considers research on how people view retirement and the many incorrect assumptions they make, some of which may keep them in jobs they dislike far longer than is healthy. Chapter 6 discusses the elements of a preretirement plan and how important it is to begin developing that plan at least two years before you actually retire. If you feel your job is in jeopardy, the chapter suggests that you begin to prepare for retirement or a job change as soon as you feel threats to your job security.

CHAPTER 5

Are You Ready to Retire?

This chapter considers research examining how people think about retirement while they are still working and the reality after they've retired. This information is especially important for those of you in the hard-worker to work-addicted range on the work addiction scale because you may be particularly surprised by the findings.

ATTITUDES ABOUT RETIREMENT

How do older people anticipate the ways in which retirement will affect their lives, and how will it differ from their working lives? Brougham and Walsh (2005) asked over 250 employees of a large university who ranged in age from 55 to 77 to indicate the relative importance of 29 goals and whether retirement or continued work would achieve those goals. This is important because it indicates a set of beliefs about what will happen to people after they retire. People in the study who were still working believed the following would take place after they retired:

1. Achievement would decline from 54 to 27 percent.
2. Contribution to the community and to greater society would decline from 40 percent to 28 percent.
3. Creativity would increase from 21 percent to 47 percent. This might suggest that jobs are currently thought of as uncreative or that people in the survey believed they'd have more time for hobbies and other creative endeavors. The researchers defined *creativity* as being curious, wanting to learn, and having original and novel ideas.

4. The quality of family lives would improve from 33 percent to 48 percent.

5. Freedom would increase from 33 percent to 68 percent.

6. Finances would decrease from 84 percent to 16 percent. The researchers defined *finances* as the ability to maintain a comfortable standard of living and have sufficient financial reserves to provide for self and family (e.g., money for a college education for children or grandchildren, emergencies, health insurance, etc.). Clearly a large majority of workers believed they'd be in much worse financial shape after retirement. How about you? What do you think?

7. Stress would increase from 28 percent to 41 percent. The researchers included the words *failure* and *guilt* in defining *stress*. It's possible that the subjects believed they'd feel guilty about not working and that the loss of work would leave them with less status.

8. Marriages would improve from 31 to 48 percent.

9. Social life and self-reliance would decrease from 58 percent to 32 percent. This might suggest that feelings of loneliness without work and loss of colleagues could affect social life.

10. Work opportunities would decrease from 81 percent to only 8 percent. The researchers defined *work opportunities* as having a rewarding job that also provided interaction with others. Clearly this group of workers believed that their social networks would diminish with retirement and that satisfying work would be difficult to find.

11. Intellectual functioning would decline from 58 percent to 35 percent. The researchers defined intellectual functioning as participation in activities that stimulated the mind and provided an opportunity to learn new skills that could be applied to a different career. The subjects may have believed that retirement would limit their motivation to learn and that without a job, new skills would not develop.

ACTUAL SATISFACTION WITH RETIREMENT

Overall Satisfaction with Retirement   Smith and Moen (2004) found that 79 percent of over 400 retirees they sampled said they were satisfied with their lives as retirees. The Health and Retirement Study (2004; http://hrson line.isr.umich.edu), including over 18,000 subjects, found that 62 percent of participants had high levels of satisfaction with retirement, while 33 percent said that they were only somewhat satisfied; only 5 percent reported dissatisfaction. The same study found that good health positively affected retirement satisfaction and that people who left jobs or careers on good terms were more satisfied with retirement than those who didn't. A national study by the RAND Corporation (2002) found the following:

A. Most people say that they are not only satisfied but "very satisfied" with retirement. In particular, people in better health and with more financial resources tend to be more satisfied (p. 15).

B. Retirees who can pay for more of their retirement expenses from lifelong guaranteed pensions (vs. accumulated savings) were more satisfied (p. 16).

C. Retirees who received some retirement planning education, had a financial advisor, or had purchased long-term care insurance were more satisfied with retirement than those who had not (p. 17).

Marital Satisfaction According to a study by Smith and Moen (2004) of over 400 retirees aged 50 to 72, 67 percent of individual spouses said that they were satisfied with retirement, while 59 percent of couples said that they were jointly satisfied. Those couples most likely to report being satisfied with retirement, individually and jointly, were retired wives and their husbands whose wives reported that their husbands were not influential in their retirement decisions. When a spouse retired and the other spouse was expected to stop work and move to a new locale, satisfaction with retirement decreased, as did, one could assume, marital satisfaction.

Stress and Mental Health Drentea (2002) analyzed data from two large national studies of retirement satisfaction with thousands of subjects. She concluded that retirement actually improves mental health because it decreases the anxiety and distress often associated with work. However, there is also evidence that working increases one's sense of control and ability to problem solve, important activities for good mental health as we age. Significantly, researchers expected to find that stress increased when people retired, but actually, stress decreased. Another important finding is that as much as people associate retirement with depression, depression actually decreased with retirement.

Bakalar (2006) reports on a study of 280 socially disadvantaged men with low-level jobs who were interviewed about life satisfaction from adolescence until an average age of 75. The researchers found that happiness in retirement didn't depend on good health or having a large income in this group of men. Men who found retirement satisfying were more than twice as likely to report enjoying relationships, volunteering, and having hobbies among their favorite activities as were those who found retirement unrewarding. Men who were unhappily retired said that they occupied their lives with what the researchers called "autistic activities" such as watching television, gambling, or caring for themselves. Forty-three percent of the happiest retirees said they found purpose in community service, while only 7 percent of those who found retirement unsatisfying did so. The researchers concluded that many of the issues that contribute to satisfaction after retirement are quite different from those that ensure a contented and economically secure middle age.

Satisfaction with Finances The financial landscape for retirees has changed dramatically because of the loss of investments as the stock market went into a tailspin in 2008, the bursting of the real estate bubble, much

higher energy costs, increases in the costs of living, and higher costs associated with health care. Some signs of things to come are found in several recent events:

   A. *Bankruptcies.* Bankruptcies among older adults have increased. Dugas (2008)
      notes that from 1991 to 2007, the rate of personal bankruptcy among those
      aged 65 or older jumped by 150 percent. The most startling rise occurred
      among those aged 75 to 84, whose bankruptcy rate soared 433 percent.
      Dugas writes, "Now, instead of going into retirement loaded with assets,
      Americans are hitting their retirement years loaded with debt." For the
      elderly, bankruptcy is a particular concern because it's typically harder for
      seniors, usually lacking well-paying job opportunities, to climb out of it.
   B. *A sinking stock market.* As the stock market tries to adjust to the new economy
      and the subprime housing troubles reduce the worth of homes, many older
      adults are seeing their savings diminish. For example, Stern (2008) writes that
      an individual with a $500,000 portfolio who experiences a 15 percent market
      decline in a year and also withdraws 7 percent of his portfolio may deplete
      the portfolio to $390,000 at the end of the first year. This requires a whop-
      ping 28 percent return just to break even at the end of the second year. One
      can see how this will make it likely that older adults who thought they were
      financially secure may find their net worth considerably reduced in a short
      period of time.

Social Satisfaction   Prince, Harwood, Blizard, and Thomas (1997) found
that available studies of adults over age 65 indicate that 5 to 15 percent
report frequently feeling lonely, and an additional 20 to 40 percent report
occasional feelings of loneliness. Among older adults over the age of 80,
50 percent often feel lonely. Sorkin, Rook, and Lu (2002) found that social isolation and loneliness decrease immune functioning and are linked to cardiovascular disease and depression. Gellene (2007) reported on a study done at
Rush Medical Center in Chicago that found that loneliness often preceded
dementia in subjects over the age of 80. The study found that the risk of
dementia increased 51 percent for every one-point increase on a five-point
scale of loneliness. The same study found that in men and women aged
50 to 67, subjects who rated themselves as very lonely had blood pressure
readings fully 30 points higher than subjects in the study who didn't rate
themselves as being lonely. Although rates of loneliness among older adults
might be higher than in other age groups because of the death of loved ones
and health problems, loneliness is a serious problem for older adults who
were either lonely before they retired or who find that the loss of work reduces their network of friendships. This may be even truer among those
who relocate after retirement and find it difficult to make friends.
   A number of writers are concerned that many of us are lonely regardless
of age. Robert Putnam (as cited in Stossel, 2000) believes that America is
developing into a country without a sense of social connectedness, where
"supper eaten with friends or family has given way to supper gobbled in

solitude, with only the glow of the television screen for companionship" (p. 1). According to Putnam,

Americans today have retreated into isolation. Evidence shows that fewer and fewer contemporary Americans are unionizing, voting, rallying around shared causes, participating in religious services, inviting each other over, or doing much of anything collectively. In fact, when we do occasionally gather—for twelve-step support encounters and the like—it's most often only as an excuse to focus on ourselves in the presence of an audience. (p. 1)

Putnam (as cited in Stossel, 2000) believes that the lack of social involvement negatively affects health, reduces tax responsibilities and charitable work, decreases productivity, and that "even simple human happiness [is] demonstrably affected by how (and whether) we connect with our family and friends and neighbors and co-workers" (p. 1). Concerns about loneliness often accompany thoughts about retirement, particularly among single people.

Satisfaction with Health   In a study of satisfaction with health, Vaillant and Mukamal (2001) found that elderly people taking three to eight medications a day who were seen as chronically ill by their physicians saw themselves as healthier than their peers. A person's positive view of life can have a significant impact on the way he perceives his physical and emotional health. This is strongly supported by a study of the physical and emotional health among a Roman Catholic order of women in the Midwest (Danner, Snowdon, & Friesen, 2001). The study found that the personal statements written by very young women as part of the admissions process to enter the religious order predicted how long they would live. The more positive and affirming the personal statements written when applicants were in their late teens and early twenties, the longer their life spans, sometimes as long as 10 years beyond the mean length of life for the religious order and up to 20 years or longer than the general population.

Many of the women in the sample lived well into their 90s and beyond. Of the 650 women in the study, 6 were over 100 years of age. Although some of the women in the sample suffered from serious physical problems, including dementia and Alzheimer's, the numbers were much smaller than the general population, and the age of onset was usually much later in life. The reasons for increased life span seem to be related to good health practices (the order doesn't permit liquor or smoking, and foods are often fresh with a focus on vegetables) and an environment that focuses on spiritual issues and helping others. The order also has a strong emphasis on maintaining a close, supportive relationship among its members so that when illnesses arise, there is a network of positive and supportive help.

In another study suggesting that optimism is the key to satisfaction with health, Jeste (2005) studied over 500 older Americans aged 60 to 98 who lived independently within the community (i.e., did not live in a nursing home or assisted care facility). Participants were asked to complete a questionnaire including medical, psychological, and demographic information. The sample was representative of national averages with regard to incidences of medical conditions (e.g., heart disease, cancer, diabetes, etc.). Similarly, 20 to 25 percent of the respondents had been diagnosed with and/or received treatment for a mental health problem. Despite the prevalence of physical illness and disabilities in the group, when participants in the study were asked to rate their own degree of successful aging on a 10-point scale, with 10 being most successful, their average rating was 8.4.

WHAT DOES THIS TELL US?

Are people satisfied with life after they retire? For the most part, yes, but what does *satisfaction* mean? Generally, it's about perception; that is, life may be awful, but if you perceive it as being good, or as good as it can be, you're likely to say you're satisfied. Researchers talk about social desirability when responding to questions about happiness, or the tendency to respond in a more positive way because doing so makes us look more successful and happy. With that in mind, let's look briefly at what researchers think contributes to happiness after retirement.

Vaillant and Mukamal (2001) found the following: (1) elderly adults who age successfully have the ability to plan ahead and are still intellectually curious and in touch with their creative abilities; (2) successfully aging adults, even those over 95, see life as being meaningful and are able to use humor in their daily lives; (3) aging successfully includes remaining physically active and continuing with activities (e.g., walking) in which a person engaged at an earlier age to remain healthy; (4) older adults who age successfully are more serene and spiritual in their outlook on life than those who age less well; and (5) successful aging includes concern for continued friendships, positive interpersonal relationships, satisfaction with loved ones and family life, and social responsibility in the form of volunteer work and civic involvement. The best evidence suggests that satisfaction as we age is a combination of good health practices, which maintain physical health; continued friendships and family interaction; a positive involvement with hobbies, volunteerism, community, and work; and a continued desire to learn and grow intellectually.

RATING YOUR OWN ATTITUDES
TOWARD RETIREMENT

To determine your readiness to retire, honestly rate your own attitudes about retirement by answering the following questions. If you've already retired, that's fine because you can use the questions to measure your current satisfaction with retirement. Answer each question on a scale ranging from 1 to 10, with 10 being the best you can be and 1 being the worst you can be. The questions pertain to what *you* think your life will be like after you retire (or for those who are retired, what life is like at present). After you answer the questions, I'll tell you what your answers mean, but no looking ahead!

1. Your level of achievement after you retire: 1–10
2. Your happiness with family life: 1–10
3. Your happiness with your marriage: 1–10
4. How happy your spouse will be after you retire: 1–10
5. How well you'll use your free time: 1–10
6. The likeliness that you'll travel: 1–10
7. Your finances: 1–10
8. Your physical health: 1–10
9. Your level of stress: 1–10
10. Your social life: 1–10
11. Your interest in developing new career opportunities: 1–10
12. Your interest in hobbies: 1–10
13. Your willingness to volunteer: 1–10
14. Your level of exercise and sports activity: 1–10
15. Your willingness to continue learning: 1–10

What Your Score Means   The total number of points you can get is 150. You need a score of at least 120 to have a positive attitude toward your life after you retire. That's an average score of at least 8 for each question. Some questions are more powerful than others. Having enough finances to retire comfortably is a very important issue. If you've scored that question very low, then you have concerns about retirement and whether you can afford it at this point. If you score well below 120, you're obviously ambivalent about retirement or you have some concerns about retirement that you need to resolve.

SUMMARY

This chapter considered research on attitudes toward retirement among workers approaching retirement age as well as attitudes of retirees toward retirement. For the most part, the research indicates that across almost every indicator, retirees are much more satisfied with retirement than they thought they would be before they actually retired. The one exception is satisfaction with finances: increasing bankruptcies, a housing decline, and a reduction in investment income have made the financial end of retirement much more troublesome for many retirees.

SUGGESTED WEB SITES

Evaluation of determinants of retirement satisfaction among workers and retired persons, http://findarticles.com/p/articles/mi_qa3852/is_200101/ai_n8928862.
Retirement satisfaction not just about income, http://behavioralhealth.typepad.com/ markhams_behavioral_healt/2006/04/retirement_sati.html.
Satisfaction and engagement in retirement, http://www.urban.org/UploadedPDF/ 311202_Perspectives2.pdf.
Three rules for retiring happy, http://money.cnn.com/2006/01/13/retirement/upde grave_money_0602/index.htm.

REFERENCES

Bakalar, N. (2006, April 4). Retirement contentment in reach for unhappy men. *New York Times.* Retrieved May 6, 2009, from http://www.nytimes.com/2006/ 04/04/health/psychology/04reti.html.
Brougham, R.R., & Walsh, D.A. (2005). Goal expectations as predictors of retirement intentions. *International Journal on Aging and Human Development, 61,* 141–160.
Danner, D.D., Snowdon, D.A., & Friesen, W.V. (2001). Positive emotions in early life and longevity: Findings from the nun study. *Journal of Personality and Social Psychology, 80,* 804–813.
Drentea, P. (2002). Retirement and mental health. *Journal of Aging and Health, 14,* 167–194.
Dugas, C. (2008, June 21). Bankruptcy seniors. *USA Today.* Retrieved May 8, 2009, from http://www.usatoday.com/money/perfi/retirement/2008-06-16-bank ruptcy-seniors_N.htm.
Gellene, D. (2007, February 10). Loneliness often precedes elder dementia, study finds. *Los Angeles Times,* p. A11.
Jeste, D. (2005, December 11–15). *Successful aging is simply "mind over matter."* Paper presented at the annual meeting of the American College of Neuropsychopharmacology, Waikoloa, Hawaii. Retrieved December 23, 2006, from http:// www.seniorjournal.com/NEWS/Aging/5-12-12-AgingMindOverMat ter.htm.
Prince, M.J., Harwood, R.H., Blizard, R.A., & Thomas, A. (1997). Social support deficits, loneliness and life events as risk factors for depression in old age: The Gospel Oak Project VI. *Psychological Medicine, 27,* 323–332.
RAND Corporation. (2002, February). *MetLife Retirement Crossroads study: Paving the way to a secure future.* Santa Monica, CA: Author.
Smith, D.B., & Moen, P. (2004). Retirement satisfaction for retirees and their spouses: Do gender and the retirement decision-making process matter? *Journal of Family Issues, 25,* 262.
Sorkin, D., Rook, K.S., & Lu, J.L. (2002). Loneliness, lack of emotional support, lack of companionship, and the likelihood of having a heart condition in an elderly sample. *Annals of Behavioral Medicine, 24,* 290–298.
Stern, L. (2008, April 28). Recession and retirement. *Newsweek, 151,* 60.
Stossel, S. (2000, September 21). Lonely in America [Interview with Robert Putnam]. *Atlantic Unbound.* Retrieved June 16, 2008, from http://www.theatlan tic.com/unbound/interviews/ba2000-11-01.htm.
Vaillant, G.E., & Mukamal, K. (2001). Successful aging. *American Journal of Psychiatry, 158*(6), 839–847.

CHAPTER 6

Developing a Preretirement Plan

Even though most workaholics don't think about retirement until it hits them, I strongly urge that those of you who tend to be even a bit work addicted think about it as early as possible. Many hardworking people begin to think about retirement, at least in passing, when they experience burnout or when the stress of their jobs begins to have physical and emotional implications. One very hardworking man told me that he began to seriously think about retirement when his hard work for an organization failed to have a payoff either in salary or promotions. What he mainly thought about was money and whether he had enough. The emotional and social aspects of retirement, however, never fully crossed his mind because he incorrectly thought they'd take care of themselves. An early retirement at age 58 with no plan at all other than sufficient savings left him feeling anxious and depressed until he decided to seek work elsewhere and found a new job. "I had nothing to do," he told me, "and after a couple of months I was climbing the walls." So that you don't end up climbing the walls, this chapter deals with early retirement planning.

YOU CAN'T BEGIN TO THINK ABOUT RETIREMENT EARLY ENOUGH

Thinking about retirement as early as possible could certainly help you have savings to retire, but does early planning actually affect other aspects of retirement? Rosenkoetter and Garris (2001) asked that question to over 600 retired people and found that those who planned the most were also the most satisfied once they retired. Those who reported no planning for retirement were inadequately prepared and reported that retirement was not what they thought it would be. The researchers also found that when retirement planning was done jointly with a spouse or mate, the adjustment to retirement was much better.

When do people begin to think seriously about retirement? It usually begins when we start to experience the signs of dissatisfaction and burnout with jobs and careers. Although this may not lead to a specific retirement plan, it does put the option on the table, and many people begin a preretirement dialogue with themselves years before they are ready to retire. What are some of the issues that might be included in your preretirement dialogue, and how might you test some of your thoughts in the real world?

ISSUES TO THINK ABOUT WELL BEFORE YOU ARE READY TO RETIRE

What Does Retirement Represent?   For many of us, retirement represents the reward at the end of a long and productive work life. It may be seen as an opportunity to rest and relax after many years of decidedly difficult work. For others, it may mean the ability to start new ventures and do many of the things we've always wanted to do but lacked the time and the income to accommodate. And for some of us, retirement is a time to grow old with nothing to look forward to.

In a study of the goals of retirees by age, Hershey, Jacobs-Lawson, and Neukam (2002) polled workers ranging in age from 20 to 67 and found that subjects felt strongly that retirement would increase their contact with others, increase leisure time, and lead to growth and creativity, regardless of age. So the first step is to rationally decide what you think retirement will lead to and test it out by understanding that if you have difficulty making friends now or have little ability to deal with leisure time, how will retirement magically improve that situation? The answer is, of course, that it won't. How do we know?

Vaillant and Mukamal (2001) found that your life style at age 50 is a solid predictor of what it will be when you retire. If you have healthy behaviors at 50, it's likely that those behaviors will continue after you retire. If you have an unhappy marriage, are prone to depression or unhappiness, have few friends, and worry a lot, chances are that these behaviors will continue after you retire unless you get some help well in advance. Retirement is not a magical cure for long-held problems, and the first thing you should do is compare your expectations for retirement with the reality of your present life. If there are areas of unhappiness or unhealthy living, it's easier to make changes before you retire, and as early as possible, than to wait until after you've retired.

An Example. Jerry Adler, age 60, is a divorced single male with a very good portfolio of investments. He is moderately happy with his job but cannot say truthfully that he likes it or that he wants to stay with it. As a typical work-addicted person with few outside interests, he uses work to stay busy, even work he doesn't particularly enjoy. In early retirement, he sees himself having more time to do many of the things he cannot do now because of the demands of work and the level of fatigue he feels during the weekend. He has few friends, few special interests, doesn't think he wants to take on a second career, and admits that he bores easily. He feels neither happy nor unhappy at present. He's thought about retirement as something he could easily move into because he has no ties to his current job or the community in which he lives.

He told me, "It's difficult for me to see myself staying in a job when I can make as much in retirement. I'd like to live someplace serene and beautiful, but I haven't thought about it much. I think about getting out of the boring life I have and hope that change will make my life better. On the retirement checklist, I had a score of 95 out of 150. I gave myself fives mostly, but eights and nines on things like finances and health. I don't think my life will be much different after I retire, except for not having to work at a job I don't like. Other things, such as meeting people and keeping busy, will take care of themselves, I think. I am who I am, and retirement isn't going to change that."

I cautioned him against taking early retirement because his lack of planning and thoughtful reflection made him a bad candidate for early retirement. Instead, I suggested preretirement workshops and planning, but he retired early nonetheless. A year later, he was back at another full-time job he didn't particularly like.

He told me, "It beats sitting home all day watching soaps, that's for sure." Had he learned anything about retirement from the experience? "Yes," he told me. "I don't have enough life skills to be retired. Work is pretty much how I spend my time. The year I spent not working was agony. I'm seeing a retirement specialist to help me plan better for those things I know I'm no good at. The retirement specialist is helping me connect with people by joining groups in town and having a better social life. It's not counseling so much as advice and practical help connecting with other people and social activities. He thinks when I'm ready for retirement that I should consider a retirement community because there are many activities and lots of ways to connect with people. I've checked them out, and they depress the hell out of me, but then maybe I'm not ready to think seriously about retirement. I was good at saving enough money for retirement but not very good about the other stuff that goes along with it. I feel like I'm getting a handle on myself, but whether it will do any good when I'm retired, I'm not sure. I still feel bored and lonely on weekends, and vacations make me miserable. I guess I have a while before I'll be ready for retirement." I agree, but at least he's working on it.

How Do You Handle Free Time?   Many of us believe incorrectly that we will handle free time well in retirement, but the way you handle free time now is a predictor of how you'll handle free time in the future. The best way to check this out is to see how long it takes you to feel bored on vacations. Many of you take work with you to prevent boredom, and some of you cut vacations short to return to work even when doing so isn't necessary. Be honest with yourself about how well you handle free time. If it's a tough question because you can't get a sense of your reaction from short vacation breaks, you may want to test the waters by taking advantage of a sabbatical and other paid leave programs available through your employer. Many companies have such programs, but often you'll need to look into them because sometimes they aren't widely advertised. Most involve developing a plan of activities that will benefit the organization, and some may involve living elsewhere.

Universities offer sabbaticals that permit faculty members to take up to two semesters off for renewal and more in-depth research on subjects associated with their academic fields. Often the first semester is at full pay, while two semesters off might reduce pay for the period to 50 percent. You are required to continue working for the organization a year or two for the length of the sabbatical or pay the sabbatical back, including benefits. Not only is this an excellent way to renew yourself and do work you've wanted to do but were too busy to complete but it's also a great way to test the waters regarding your ability to handle free time.

Organizations sometimes offer a phased retirement in which you have as long as five years to reduce the number of hours you work, with the difference made up through use of your pension. For example, the California State University system allows faculty members to retire, receive their full pension, and teach up to a 50 percent load for five years. Many faculty members use this as a way to transition to full retirement, but it also has financial benefits because pensions may not fully cover all your living expenses. While the faculty member works, social security benefits increase so that when the phased retirement program ends, final social security benefits have grown considerably.

An Example. One example of someone who used a sabbatical to test the retirement waters is Robert Benson, a 59-year-old middle manager for a Kansas City software firm who liked his job but was worn out from many years of very hard work and long hours, and needed a break. There was no sabbatical policy to provide him the needed time to renew himself after an extraordinary run of very demanding work assignments. Robert and his wife wanted to travel and take time off from a work life that was quickly affecting his health because of the high level of stress. His option was to resign, take his savings, and rest until he needed to find another job. In a long conversation with his wife, an alternative plan was developed that he would share with his boss.

The plan was to propose a differential-in-pay leave. Robert would find a replacement for his job who would work at a salary somewhat lower than Robert's. In some organizations, that amount would be up to half of the normal salary. Robert would advertise the position as a way to gain new experience for people like him who were looking for a break from current jobs. As an added incentive, he would offer to rent his house to the new person for a nominal fee. The house would be empty anyway, and finding a responsible short-term renter would help financially and set his mind at ease about the care of his house.

As an incentive to the company, Robert promised to do marketing research in his travels and to return with a comprehensive report at the end of his leave. The company agreed that Robert needed a break and agreed to pay the differential salary to the new person as long as Robert found a person suitable for the job. Because Robert was well connected, he was soon able to find an out-of-work colleague with excellent qualifications to work in Robert's place for the year of his leave. The agreement was that Robert would receive half salary and full benefits during the year and that he would then return to his position full-time. Robert's replacement would receive the other half of Robert's salary, a considerable improvement over unemployment compensation. If the replacement worked out, there would be an attempt to find him full-time work in the company or in an allied company.

Robert spent a blissful time traveling for a year. It wasn't easy at first because it had been years since Robert had a real vacation when he hadn't worked as much during the vacation as he did on the job. His wife helped by keeping them very busy and having a number of activities worked out before the sabbatical began. Robert used to be an avid tennis player before work all but consumed him. His wife had him join the United States Tennis Association, and through that organization's system of helping people find tennis partners, everywhere they went, Robert played tennis and made new friends.

At the end of the year, he found himself renewed and ready to return to work with a full head of steam. His report saved the company much more than it may have lost in the arrangement, and his replacement now has a job with the company. These creative arrangements are possible in even the worst of business climates if you are willing to think through arrangements that benefit all parties involved.

Did the sabbatical help Robert with preretirement planning? "Yes," he told me. "Had I not taken a sabbatical, the chances of my successfully retiring would have been very poor. Had I retired early as I often thought I would, I would have been a mess. I'd forgotten how to enjoy life. My only thoughts before the sabbatical were about work. Having a more leisurely year behind me, I've started thinking seriously about retirement. I know I have some work to do to make it happen successfully, but I think I've gained some skills I'd lost, and I think they'd serve me well in retirement."

This is not to say that phased retirement through sabbaticals and early retirement programs completely eliminate the need to prepare people to handle free time or make formerly hardworking retirees more satisfied with full retirement. Reitzes and Mutran (2004) followed people in a phased retirement program for two years before retirement and two years after they retired. What they found was confirmation of Atchley's (1975, 1982) five stages of adjustment to retirement: (1) the *honeymoon period*, which is characterized as a euphoric period in which retirees relish their new freedom of time and space; (2) the *disenchantment period*, which reflects the emotional letdown as people face the reality of everyday life in retirement; (3) the *reorientation period*, which refers to the development of a realistic view of the social and economic opportunities and constraints of retirement; (4) the *stability period*, which occurs when people have achieved a certain accommodation and adjustment to retirement; and (5) the *termination period*, which denotes the eventual loss of independence because of illness and disability.

Reitzes and Mutran (2004) also found that (1) preretirement self-esteem and a rich social network as well as pension eligibility, increased positive attitudes toward retirement throughout the 24-month period following retirement, and (2) retirement planning and voluntary retirement increased positive attitudes toward retirement in the initial period of retirement but not later in the first two years of retirement. After the honeymoon period wore off, retirees had to deal with the realities of retirement that weren't completely understood during their phased-in preretirement period. Those realities include unscheduled time, boredom, loss of status, fewer social contacts, and lack of useful engagement in work or other activities to remain busy.

The reason that hardworking and often work-addicted people go through Atchley's phases is that retirement without work is a shock. We often think of work in its least satisfying way as a chore, something to do to provide us with food and shelter, but work gives us meaning. It also offers status, helps us fill our time, and provides, at its best, intense satisfaction and friendships. This is why the next area of planning is to think about some form of continued work after retirement, but work that is satisfying and perhaps new and innovative.

Should You Continue to Work after You Retire? According to Zedlewski and Butrica (2007), research evidence increasingly shows that older adults who regularly work after retirement enjoy better health and live longer, thanks to stimulating environments and a sense of purpose. Calvo (2006) found that paid work for older adults improves health. Tsai, Wendt, Donnelly, de Jong, and Ahmed (2005) followed a sample of early retirees for 30 years and found that they died earlier than workers who retired later. Dhaval, Rashad, and Spasojevic (2006) report that complete retirement without work decreases physical and emotional health.

The reasons why work improves health are that it increases brain activity, exposure to stimulating challenges, and social interactions with others (Kubzansky, Berkman, & Seeman, 2000); increases social status (Thoits &

Hewitt, 2001); and offers greater access to social, psychological, and material resources (Wilson, 2000). Some work-related activities help older adults develop knowledge and skills that boost their self-image and mental outlook (Harlow-Rosentraub, Wilson, & Steele, 2006).

Once older adults reach age 65, most will opt for retirement (Ekerdt, 1998). Although some individuals move from full-time work to full-time leisure, a substantial number remain in the labor force after they leave their career jobs (Hansson, DeKoekkoek, Neece, & Patterson, 1997). Many of these working-retired adults are in bridge-type jobs that help them transition from long-term career positions to total retirement (Feldman, 1994; Mutchler, Burr, Pienta, & Massagli, 1997). "Bridge jobs may be part-time work, self-employment, or temporary work, and often involve a combination of fewer hours, less stress or responsibility, greater flexibility, and fewer physical demands" (Feldman, 1994, p. 286).

Ulrich and Brott (2005) studied the strategies made by retirees to transition into bridging jobs. The following themes emerged: (1) most retirees studied had planned for finances but had made no plans for their social and work lives following retirement and hadn't used retirement planning or thought about job resources; (2) some didn't have to start over again because they had marketable skills and good reputations; (3) many people discovered that work after retirement was characterized by negative changes, including lower pay, problems finding compatible colleagues at work, and limited responsibility when compared to former jobs; (4) many found the loss of status in bridge jobs hard to take; (5) many failed to look at jobs as they would prior to retirement and in time were disappointed with their bridge jobs; (6) many didn't consider bridge jobs because they felt that they had limited technological skills for the job or that they couldn't learn new skills; (7) many found employment-related tests to be demeaning, believing that high job achievement before retirement negated the need for testing; (8) many thought that age discrimination affected both their preretirement jobs and bridge jobs and noted that younger employees often questioned their ability to do the job; and (9) regardless of these challenges, retirees benefited considerably from their bridge jobs. They credited their bridge jobs with making them feel better about themselves while giving them a more balanced life and helping them enjoy their work. They also felt better about themselves because they continued to learn, made a difference to others, were able to demonstrate their competency, and felt healthy.

However, the option to retire early or even to retire when you are ready may be outside your control. A study by Rampell & Saltmarsh (2009) indicated that in the United States, almost one-third of people aged 65 to 69 were still in the labor force; in France, just 4 percent of people this age were still working or looking for work. The same study found that nearly 4 in 10 workers over age 62 said they had delayed their retirement because of the recession.

An Example. Janet Ebberly, a 65-year-old Palm Springs social worker, thought she was about as burned out as she could be from a highly demanding job in child protective services working with abused children, often 12 to 14 hours a day and many weekends when she was on call. She and her husband (a physician in private practice) thought about retirement as a way to reduce the stress in their lives through travel and personal growth, but a year of complete retirement from work suggested that she wasn't ready to stop working. When her employer asked her to return to work part-time, she jumped at the chance and is now very happy working two and a half days a week.

I asked her why she had initially thought retirement would be so much better than work. She told me, "This may sound strange coming from someone who works with people and knows a lot about human behavior, but we were so caught up in our careers and the stress from our jobs that we never really thought about retirement as anything but a respite from stress. We thought we'd be older than we actually are. I mean we thought we'd feel old when in fact we feel young. We thought we'd have health problems at age 65 but, thank God, we're both very healthy. We thought travel would be glamorous and exciting, and it was for maybe a month, but then it just became boring. We should have taken long trips before we retired or worked part-time or done something to test out how we dealt with free time, but we didn't.

"The reality is that neither one of us likes a lot of free time, and going back to work part-time has been wonderful. I work the first two and a half days of the week and John works the second two and a half days so we have what feels like a normal workweek. Before we went back to work part-time, we were getting into each other's hair, and it was annoying. Now we feel grateful to have each other evenings and weekends, and we plan trips and have our dreams, but they're a lot more realistic. I would say that a reality check should be done throughout your adult life to check your thinking about retirement. Be honest with yourself, because we weren't, and it led to a very troubled and unhappy year for us until we went back to work."

So yes, the evidence seems to suggest that some form of work is preferable to no work at all once you retire, but under these circumstances, work should include a very wide range of definitions: part-time work, consulting, self-employment, a new career, reduced hours on a current job, and other creative options.

Is Work So Bad That You Need to Quit and Consider Retirement as an Option?   Older workers often have little choice in whether they continue working full-time. As Mor-Barak and Tynan (1993) point out, "Despite this interest in continued employment by employers and older adults, older workers are more likely to lose their jobs than younger workers in instances such as plant closings and corporate mergers" (p. 45). The authors go on to say that many businesses can't or won't deal with life events faced by older workers such as "widowhood and caring for ailing spouses, and as a result many older workers are forced to retire earlier than planned" (p. 45).

Writing about the loss of work and its impact on older men, Levant (1997) says that as men lose their good-provider roles, the experience results in "severe gender role strain" (p. 221), which affects relationships and can be disruptive to the point of ending otherwise strong marriages. Because older adults are more likely to lose high-level jobs as a result of downsizing and age discrimination, social contacts decrease, and many otherwise healthy and motivated workers must deal with increased levels of isolation and loneliness in retirement. Schneider (1998) points out that many of us are workaholics and that when work is taken away or jobs are diminished in complexity and creativity, many older adults experience a decrease in physical and mental health. And though early retirement is touted as a way to achieve the good life while still young, the experience is a complex and even wrenching one, in which older adults who are financially able to retire often have little ability to handle extra time, have failed to make sound retirement plans, and find out quickly that not working takes away social contacts, status, and a way to organize time.

For many healthy, work-oriented, and motivated older adults, volunteer and civic roles are not at all what they are looking for. They want to continue to work, to contribute, and to receive the financial and social status and benefits related to work. A troubled economy and the loss of investments and equity in housing suggest that the American workplace will see many older workers continue to work well into their 70s and beyond. However, a longer work life has negative ramifications for workers who have worked at physically and emotionally demanding jobs and have seen their bodies wear out.

In an analysis of the impact of paid work and formal volunteerism, Zedlewski and Butrica (2007) found that numerous studies support the finding that work and formal volunteering improve health, reduce the risk of serious illness and emotional difficulties such as depression, and improve strength and cognitive functioning. However, full retirement without work and the early loss of a job increased the probability of illness and emotional difficulties. Having something of value to do after retirement helps keep older adults healthy and emotionally engaged with the world around them.

An Example. Jerry Paulson is someone who likes his Chicago civil engineering job and has no plans to retire early. He told me:

I'm 68, and I still feel a high when I go to work. I'm well taken care of financially, and my wife keeps telling me we could see the world instead of my continuing to work, but to be truthful, I don't really want to see the world, and she knows it. I like the folks I work with and the work is fun. I get razzed a lot about being too old to do the job, but everyone knows how good I am at it. I see a lot of my friends who retired early and stopped working full-time before they were ready, and they're miserable. They didn't like their jobs, and I told them that maybe doing something else would make the difference, but now they work at part-time jobs that pay next to nothing. One of them greets people at Wal-Mart. He's a smart guy who was a very successful appraiser but unhappy at his job, and now he greets people. I know that he hates it. He quit his job because he was burned out and wishes he was back at it, but with the current housing market in shambles, he can't find anything else to do. I think planning for work after you retire is a necessity, and if you like your job and you can keep working, I'd recommend that people do it. When I actually do retire, we'll be very comfortable financially. Just working these few years past 65 has made a real difference in our savings.

Will You Be Financially Secure in Retirement?   The economy in 2008, 2009, and 2010 has led to a reversal in the value of homes and investments, and many older people who had hoped to retire early are now faced with too little money to retire. My heart goes out to all of us who worked hard and thought we were financially secure only to discover how vulnerable we can be when the economy suffers a cataclysmic reversal. I'm optimistic that the economy will rebound, but until then, it's important that you find competent people to help you manage your money. I know that some of you are excellent money managers and don't need outside help, but speaking for myself and many others who aren't, I have found that skilled financial advisors can be a real help, particularly when managing money requires a sure hand and expertise I and many others lack. In good times, everyone is a hero, but in bad times, the very good people are the ones who can pull us out of financial disasters.

For that reason, I strongly suggest that you seek out the best people you can find. Most financial advisors charge about 1 percent to manage your investments, but others receive commissions from mutual funds. I'm not keen on this latter approach because it encourages selling and buying of funds just for the sake of making a commission. Be certain that your financial advisor has fiduciary responsibility to you. In other words, ensure that the advisor always works for you and for your best interests and doesn't have competing relationships with mutual funds or other investment organizations. I also suggest that you find very good real estate people who can help you properly evaluate the worth of your home and its potential to grow value in the coming years. They can also make suggestions about renovations and simple improvements that might substantially increase the value of your home.

An Example. Oscar Larson is a 68-year-old former university professor who taught at the University of North Dakota for over 40 years. Oscar had planned to retire on what he thought was a healthy mix of investments, a state pension, and Social Security. He also had a house valued at about $250,000 before the real estate crash in 2008. The investments lost half their worth since 2008 and have failed to come back very much from their 2007 highs. Oscar was invested in highly aggressive growth stocks and mutual funds. When the crash came, they did badly. His house lost $100,000 in value, and the real estate market is so bad where he lives that he has no hope of selling it, even at a loss. He had wanted to move somewhere warm but just cannot afford it right now. He doesn't want to take money from his investments, and Social Security and his state pension only provide about 70 percent of what he needs to live on.

Oscar found out through the university grapevine about a very competent financial advisor who immediately put his investments in more age-appropriate and safer stocks, bonds, and mutual funds. His investments have come back about 25 percent from their initial low. He thinks he might recoup much of what he lost in the next year or two using his financial advisor. He also spoke to a very good real estate agent who helped him rent his home. With the rent and the tax deduction from the rental, he breaks even. He has found a rental in a retirement community for less than his mortgage payments in North Dakota and can now live in a warmer climate, although his budget is tight. If his investments come back, by the time he takes his mandatory withdrawals from his 403(b) at age 70 and a half, he should have a much healthier income and hopes to buy a house. In the meantime, to supplement his income, he's working part-time at a local junior college in Arizona. He didn't think he'd continue teaching but finds the added income a strong incentive, and he likes the students and the courses he teaches.

Even in a down economic time, you can make necessary adjustments to have financial security, but you need to use the very best people available and not the salespeople who often come to your workplace, know nothing about investments, and may put you in jeopardy by selling investments that have great short-term gains but are real losers in the long run.

Oscar told me,

I worked very hard, put as much money as I could into tax-deferred [403(b)] investments at the state university I worked at, and then saw much of it lost in just a few months in 2008. It completely messed up my retirement plans to move to Arizona and live in an academic retirement community near friends I had taught with. I found a place in Arizona where I live cheaply but it's not what I'd hoped for. It hurt like hell, and I was really angry for a long time, until I began to seek out highly competent people. Had I not been so busy, I'd have sought them out earlier in my career, but like a lot of us workaholics, I only had time for work. I had this really dumb belief that thinking about money was beneath me since, as an academic, I was doing such important work. Well, the most important work I could have done was taking care of myself and not buying into the BS of the people who'd come by my office to sell me investments. I'd figured if the university let them in, they must be good. What a dumb idea that was. Most of them knew nothing about the market and were just trying to make a lot of money on the correct assumption that those of us in the ivory tower would be too busy, too arrogant, or too dumb about money to think twice about what they were selling us. And they were right.

I was good at making and saving my money but awful at growing it. Find someone good to give you advice about your investments—even if it costs a bit extra—listen to them, work closely with them so you can keep tabs on their investment philosophy, and be a critical and sophisticated consumer. I've begun reading some very good financial magazines and the *Wall Street Journal*. I want to know what's going on. The more I've read, the more interesting the subject has become. I've gone from a complete financial bonehead to someone who can talk to my financial advisor in a knowledgeable way. We work together, and I've seen evidence of how much my investments have come back in a short period of time to know that had I done this when I was younger, I'd be a fairly well-off man today instead of someone living too close to the vest to be entirely comfortable. Even workaholics need to take the time to put their talents to work to grow their money so that when they burn out or when their health gets bad and they need a break, they're in good financial shape.

SUMMARY

In this chapter, I discussed issues related to planning for retirement and suggested that you begin planning early enough to test the waters by considering whether you want to work longer, whether your work still gives you pleasure, how you handle free time, and whether you will be financially secure. This is a process that takes time and evolves. Trying to answer these questions a short time before you retire is unwise because this process may take several years or more and involve examining behaviors and situations that are new to you.

SUGGESTED WEB SITES

How to retire in style, http://www.fool.com/Retirement/RetirementPlanning/RetirementPlanning01.htm.

Planning for retirement: Top 10 things to know, http://money.cnn.com/magazines/moneymag/money101/lesson13/.

Planning for retirement: Your "to do" planner for a smooth transition, http://www.todaysseniors.com/pages/planning_for_retirement.html.

Planning your retirement, http://www.usnews.com/Topics/tag/Series/p/planning_your_retirement/index.html.

Taking the mystery out of retirement, http://www.dol.gov/ebsa/publications/nearretirement.html.

REFERENCES

Atchley, R. C. (1975). Adjustment to the loss of job at retirement. *International Journal of Aging and Human Development, 6*, 17–27.

Atchley, R. C. (1982). Retirement: Learning the world of work. *Annals of the American Academy of Political and Social Sciences, 464*, 120–131.

Calvo, E. (2006). Does working longer make people healthier and happier? In *Work Opportunities for Older Americans* (Series 2). Chestnut Hill, MA: Center for Retirement Research, Boston College.

Dhaval, D., Rashad, I., & Spasojevic, J. (2006). *The effects of retirement on physical and mental health outcomes*. NBER Working Paper No. 12123. Cambridge, MA: NBER.

Ekerdt, D. (1998). Workplace norms for the timing of retirement. In K. Schaie & C. Schooler (Eds.), *Impact of work on older adults* (pp. 101–123). New York: Springer.

Feldman, D. C. (1994). The decision to retire early: A review and conceptualization. *Academy of Management Review, 19*, 285–311.

Hansson, R.O., DeKoekkoek, P. D., Neece, W.M., & Patterson, D. W. (1997). Successful aging at work: Annual review, 1992–1996: The older worker and transition to retirement. *Journal of Vocational Behavior, 51*, 202–233.

Harlow-Rosentraub, K., Wilson, L., & Steele, J. (2006). Expanding youth service concepts for older adults: Americorps results. In L. Wilson & S. Simson (Eds.), *Civic engagement and the baby boomer generation: Research, policy and practice perspectives* (pp. 61–84). New York: Haworth Press.

Hershey, D.A., Jacobs-Lawson, J. M., & Neukam, K.A. (2002). Influences of age and gender on workers' goals for retirement. *International Journal of Aging and Human Development, 55*, 163–179.

Kubzansky, L. D., Berkman, L. F., & Seeman, T. E. (2000). Social conditions and distress in elderly persons: Findings from the MacArthur Studies of Successful Aging. *Journals of Gerontology: Psychological Science, 55b*, 238–246.

Levant, R. F. (1997). The masculinity issue. *Journal of Men's Studies, 5*, 221–229.

Mor-Barak, M. E., & Tynan, M. (1993, January). Older workers and the workplace: A new challenge for occupational social work. *Social Work, 38*, 45–55.

Mutchler, J. E., Burr, J.A., Pienta, A. M., & Massagli, M.P. (1997). Pathways to labor force exit: Work transitions and work instability. *Journals of Gerontology: Social Sciences, 52b*, S4–S12.

Rampell, K., & Saltmarsh, M. (2009). *A reluctance to retire means fewer openings.* Retrieved September 3, 2009, from http://www.nytimes.com/2009/09/03/business/03retire.html?th&emc=th.

Reitzes, D. C., & Mutran, E. J. (2004). The transition to retirement: Stages and factors that influence retirement adjustment. *International Journal of Aging and Human Development, 59*, 63–84.

Rosenkoetter, M. M., & Garris, J. M. (2001). Postretirement use of time: Implications for preretirement planning and postretirement management. *Issues in Mental Health Nursing, 22*, 703–722.

Schneider, K. J. (1998). Toward a science of the heart: Romanticism and the revival of psychology. *American Psychologist, 53*, 277–289.

Tsai, S. P., Wendt, J. K., Donnelly, R.P., de Jong, G., & Ahmed, F.S. (2005). Age at retirement and long-term survival of an industrial population: Prospective cohort study. *British Medical Journal, 331*, 995–1004.

Ulrich, L. B., & Brott, P. E. (2005, December). Older workers and bridge employment: Redefining retirement. *Journal of Employment Counseling, 42*, 159–170.

Vaillant, G.E., & Mukamal, K. (2001). Successful aging. *American Journal of Psychiatry, 158*, 839–847.

Wilson, J. (2000). Volunteering. *Annual Review of Sociology, 26*, 215–240.

Zedlewski, S. R., & Butrica, B. A. (2007, December). Are we taking full advantage of older adults' potential? In *The Retirement Project: Perspectives of productive aging* (p. 9). Washington, D.C: Urban Institute.

PART III

The Retirement Decision

Chapters 7 and 8 discuss making the actual decision to retire. Chapter 7 shows how family and friends can be very helpful in listening to your retirement plans and providing feedback. Chapter 8 goes through the actual retirement plan and provides suggestions on how to move from your pretirement plan to the one you'll implement as you approach retirement.

CHAPTER 7

Involving Family Members in Retirement Decisions

Many of us who have worked very hard much of our lives have to some degree alienated our families and loved ones by not being available and by having distant relationships. As you approach retirement, it's very important that you try to reconnect with family. Not only can they be helpful in the transition to retired life but many retired people find that better family relationships can be one of the most satisfying aspects of retired life. In this chapter, I'll discuss ways that families and loved ones can help in the transition from full-time work to retired life.

RETIREMENT AFFECTS FAMILY LIFE

Retirement affects everyone in a family. For that reason, you should talk over your plans with your extended family, including your friends. Many of them may have stereotypes of retired living that are untrue, unrealistic, or don't apply to you. It's important that you deal with these misconceptions so that you have a supportive family and a core of understanding friends to help you move toward and into retirement. Some issues that family members may wish to discuss openly with you include the following: (1) your children may be concerned that you will spend too much time with them; (2) your spouse may worry that with extra time on your hands, you might demand a great deal of his or her time and attention; (3) concerns may exist over whether you will have enough money and, in the event of your death, how your estate will be dealt with and whether it will be apportioned fairly; and (4) friends may see you as being very active and wonder if you'll be able to handle this extra leisure time. These are all legitimate issues to consider, and your response should be thoughtful, measured, and honest.

We sometimes believe that children and family members will let us down as we age, particularly when we are in need of physical and emotional assistance, but Glaser, Stuchbury, Tomasine, and Askham (2008) found that to the contrary, children often help out when older adult marriages dissolve or in the event of the death of a spouse. The researchers indicated that although much of the current literature points to distancing by family members if a retired loved one divorces, the researchers found a changing attitude toward the divorcing parent who remarries, and as much help is given when needed to that parent as when the parent was still married to his long-term mate.

Nuttman-Schwartz (2007) suggests the importance of involving family members in early retirement planning. The researcher writes, "The results [of the study] showed family perceptions contribute to postretirement adjustment. Thus, in order to help the retirees to accept their retirement transition, it suggests that the pre-retirement intervention should focus on the family as a whole, especially when retirees plan their future" (p. 192). According to the author, preplanning with family is particularly important when the retiree shows signs of loneliness and depression before retirement because these emotional states may continue and even worsen after retirement.

Carpenter, Rickdeschel, Van Haitsma, and Feldman (2006) found that adult children sometimes know their parents' preferences for retired life but are often unaware of many important issues, particularly those issues that pertain to achieving a high quality of life. The researchers suggest that families engage themselves in discussions of late-life issues and find out about parental preferences. The authors recognize that families may not have these discussions "because of time constraints, discomfort bringing up topics that imply eventual impairment, or simply because families lack the tools to have productive discussions about preferences" (p. 562). The authors suggest a family process to reevaluate and accommodate the changing needs and preferences of older adults as they consider and move into retirement. The researchers conclude by saying that "because most children inevitably play some role in guiding the psychosocial care of their parents, it is imperative to find ways to improve their knowledge about parent preferences and values" (p. 562).

ADVICE FOR FAMILY MEMBERS

The first thing family members need to know is that the entire notion of retirement is anxiety provoking for many retirees, primarily because it may suggest that productive life is over and that a gradual decline in health and life satisfaction is about to occur. It may also initiate fears about financial instability and boredom. So don't be surprised if your loved ones have fears and unrealistic expectations or if they just don't want to talk about retirement. All these reactions are common and are increasingly important to discuss as the person moves closer to making the decision to retire. Your support can be very helpful. Calm listening and trying to understand the retiree's concerns are the best antidotes to preretirement anxiety. Attacking ideas or perceptions or saying that you've read negative things about the decisions a loved one is considering is never a good way to show that you care or that you want to help. There is no better way to find out about retirement than reading good research-oriented articles and talking to older adults you respect who have gone through what your loved one is going through.

Early retirement is a particularly difficult decision to make because it often comes when older adults are burned out on work or have enough money saved so that work isn't really necessary. Most of the research suggests that people who retire early have issues related to boredom and are less satisfied than their later-retiring counterparts. This isn't always the case, but it's a finding to think about. What the early retiree might need is a break from work to get over stress and to get her creative juices flowing again. The best advice to loved ones considering early retirement is to keep their options open.

An Example. I spoke to a hospital administrator who had retired recently at age 62. Clearly he was burned out over the increasingly stressful job of trying to keep a hospital afloat while hearing constant complaints from patients and doctors and struggling with insurance companies to get bills paid. He told me he had no desire to work again and said that he was fully occupied with hiking, mountain bike riding, and seeing his grandchildren. He kept chatting long after I was finished playing tennis, and I had the feeling that as burned out as he no doubt was, he had a lot more work left in him. I suggested that he keep his options open just in case he needed something to do at some point. He mulled it over and said that he had many options if he got bored and that maybe he'd pursue them. I thought that was a wise decision. You don't go from running a multi-million-dollar hospital to taking care of grandkids overnight without some potential for boredom.

I wondered how his children felt about his plan to see them more frequently. He said they were happy about it, hesitated, and then said he *assumed* they were happy about it but hadn't discussed it in any depth with them. I thought it would be a good idea if he did. He told me a week later that while his kids sounded happy about his plan to visit often, there was a subtle suggestion that it ought not be *too* often or *too* long. He was surprised and a little hurt but guessed it was better to find out now instead of later and went on to discuss a part-time work possibility he had, and how he thought maybe a couple months of doing nothing might get him back in the mood to work again—but nothing, he added, as stressful as his work as a hospital administrator. He said, "The American health care system is tilting toward being broken and trying to keep things together is a job I never want to tackle again." He also admitted that he was divorced and a bit lonely and that maybe finding a mate was what he should do instead of spending too much time with his grandkids. He asked if I knew any eligible single women in town. Yes, I said, I did, and I'd chat with them first, and if they wanted to follow up, I'd give them his name and he or they could call. Amazing what people tell you at the tennis courts.

Why would such a high-level person have such a limited retirement plan? Not having a spouse or mate with whom to discuss his plan is certainly one reason. When you're single, you get used to making your own decisions without consulting others. Burnout drove his retirement decision, and that's never a good motivator to retire because often when we leave the situation causing burnout, our energy and drive return, and then what? Finally, he needed to chat about his plans in a quiet and ongoing way with his children. He admitted that most of the talking he'd done about retirement was initiated during family reunions when people were happy and a little drunk and that this was no time to talk about serious matters. I agreed.

I would also suggest that family members attend preretirement seminars with you. Being able to talk about the material in the seminars with family members helps process how you will approach a number of retirement issues. Even though you may not be ready to retire, attending preretirement seminars a year or two before you intend to retire gives you time to consider and plan for the many issues that retirement presents, including where to live; whether you want to continue working; financial stability; spending more time with your children; understanding Social Security, other pensions, and Medicare; and having your health fully evaluated and any medical issues dealt with.

Hershey, Mowen, and Jacobs-Lawson (2003) found that preretirement seminars focusing on financial issues had a positive impact on financial planning but that carryover of learning often required a family member or friend to be present to reinforce what had been covered for it to have a lasting impact. The authors write, "Clearly, one of the more prominent takeaway messages from this investigation is that a relatively brief financial information intervention can have a positive effect on retirement planning, goal-setting, and savings practices" (p. 555).

Discussing the complex issues that affect married couples when one spouse is considering retirement, Pienta (2003) writes, "As more married couples enter their pre-retirement years, complex work and family issues will rise to the surface" (p. 355). Some of these issues include age differences in working couples when the wife (or husband) has more years to work before retirement than the retiring spouse and how that affects retirement plans and retirement satisfaction. Another issue is that the younger working spouse will probably bring in more money than the retired spouse. Will this create problems in the relationship? Large age differences in spouses sometimes mean that the younger spouse may become a caretaker of the older spouse while the younger spouse is still working, upsetting the younger spouse's retirement plans. Being together much of the time after retirement sometimes creates its own set of problems. Issues relating to money and inheritances may create considerable family antagonism. For these reasons, Pienta suggests the use of retirement counselors to help with future and ongoing issues related to retirement. Even though few people utilize retirement counselors at present (Turner, Bailey, & Scott, 1994), I think it's a very good idea in that specially trained retirement counselors can resolve problems that are difficult to anticipate but that seriously affect the couple.

SUMMARY

This chapter discussed the importance of involving loved ones in the retirement decision as well as your retirement plans. Several studies are reported showing that children and other family members can be very involved in retirement planning and can help with difficult retirement decisions. The chapter strongly advises that preretirement seminars be attended with family members so that the often-complicated issues discussed in seminars can be processed with loved ones. Several examples were provided showing the need for family and professional help to resolve retirement issues including burnout, loss of retirement income, and boredom. Several examples were provided of preretirement issues involving loss of investment money to pay for retirement, boredom, burnout, and problems related to early retirement.

SUGGESTED WEB SITES

Is retirement different for women?, http://www.foxbusiness.com/story/personal-finance/retirement-different-women-309979094/.

Older worker, families and public policy, http://www.aifs.gov.au/institute/pubs/fm/fm53iw2.pdf.

Retirement influences on marital and family relations, http://family.jrank.org/pages/1406/Retirement-Retirement-Influences-on-Marital-Family-Relations.html.

Seniors and the Internet: Consuming technology to enhance life and family involvement, http://www.crito.uci.edu/noah/HOIT/HOIT%20Papers/Seniors%20and%20the%20Internet.pdf.

Transition issues for the elderly and their families, http://www.ec-online.net/knowledge/Articles/brandttransitions.html.

REFERENCES

Carpenter, B.D., Rickdeschel, K., Van Haitsma, K.S., & Feldman, P.H. (2006, December). Adult children as informants about parent's psychosocial preferences. *Family Relations, 55,* 552–563.

Glaser, K., Stuchbury, R., Tomasine, C., & Askham, J. (2008). The long-term consequences of partnership dissolution for support in later life in the United Kingdom, *Aging and Society,* 329–351.

Hershey, D.A., Mowen, J.C., & Jacobs-Lawson, J.M. (2003). An experimental comparison of retirement planning intervention seminars. *Educational Gerontology, 339*, 339–359.

Nuttman-Schwartz, O. (2007, April/June). Men's perception of family during the retirement transition. *Families in Society, 88*, 192–202.

Pienta, A.M. (2003). Partners in marriage: An analysis of husbands' and wives' retirement behavior. *Journal of Applied Gerontology, 22*, 340–361.

Turner, M.J., Bailey, W.C., & Scott, J.P. (1994). Factors influencing attitude toward retirement and retirement planning among midlife university employees. *Journal of Applied Gerontology, 13*, 143–156.

CHAPTER 8

The Decision to Retire

A number of researchers confirm that making the decision to retire can be very difficult, particularly for those who have spent their entire career in high-pressure jobs with endless hours of work. Although it is often assumed that retirement is a pleasant experience, and for many people it is, the process of retiring can be daunting and the decision itself so difficult to make that about 30 percent of all retirees perceive it as being very stressful (Atchley, 1975; Bossé, Aldwin, Levenson, & Workman-Daniels, 1991; Braithwaite, Gibson, & Bosly-Craft, 1986).

The reasons for retirement stress are easy enough to understand. Even though you may be emotionally and physically ready to retire, moving into the unknown after years of investing yourself in work can be very demanding. There are many aspects of retirement that even the best planning can't anticipate, and predictably many people find the entire process stressful. Many hard workers prepare to enter retirement when they aren't emotionally ready because they've been forced into retirement by cutbacks and downsizing and have no alternatives. Worker burnout and job unhappiness give many workers a false sense that retirement will help rid them of bad feelings about work when this is often far from the case. Additionally, retiring because of poor health often leads to even more retirement stress.

Forced retirement or retirement arising when workers are given strong messages that they are unwanted have both been associated with greater difficulties in adjusting to retirement (Atchley, 1982; Walker, Kimmel, & Price, 1981), lower satisfaction with retirement (Isaksson, 1997), adverse psychological reactions (Sharpley & Layton, 1998), and increased stress (Isaksson, 1997; Sharpley & Layton, 1998).

Workers who are forced to retire because of ill health predictably report lower levels of morale (Braithwaite et al., 1986), higher stress scores (Bossé et al., 1991), and are at greater risk for emotional difficulties (Sharpley & Layton, 1998). Martin-Matthews and Brown (1988) found that the lower the socioeconomic status of men, the more negative the impact of retirement overall, often because of a lack of planning, lower postretirement income, early health problems, and few alternatives to work. Workers who experience a substantial loss of income during retirement tend to experience poor morale (Richardson & Kilty, 1991) and poor adjustment (Palmore, Fillenbaum, & George, 1984). Many people who find their retirement plans changed because companies no longer honor pension plans or have grossly changed these plans also report lower satisfaction with retirement and greater levels of emotional stress.

Fletcher and Hansson (1991) report that retirees who expected to have very little personal control over their lives during retirement not only had more negative views of retirement but also feared the event. Glamser (1976) found that those expecting retirement to be a positive experience held a positive attitude about retirement, while those expecting retirement to be a negative adjustment held negative attitudes.

Early retirement is a complex issue for many older adults who may feel unappreciated and mistreated at work and see retirement as a way of coping with low morale and stress. Often retirement isn't a solution because many early retirees haven't thought through retirement as a lifestyle change and may still desire to work in new organizations but may believe that their age makes new employment unlikely. Financial incentive plans for early retirement that seem lucrative may in fact offer a person less financial security in the long run and reduce Social Security and pension benefits. Work is important to most people because it offers status and a daily schedule. When these two factors are taken away, many early retirees feel unimportant and confused about how to spend their day. As a nurse told a colleague when he began chatting about his plan to retire early, "You have 30 good years ahead of you. What are you going to do with yourself?" She was absolutely right, and my colleague decided to handle his unhappiness with a current job by finding a job elsewhere. This gave him two more years of work while he began careful planning for retirement and increased his savings.

Mor-Barak and Tynan (1993) suggest that retirement at 65 is an "artifact of the Social Security laws" that make retirement around 65 seem normal, when many workers may wish to continue working long past that age. They also believe that the 65-year retirement age allows companies to rid themselves of otherwise faithful workers by developing a culture within the organization that encourages early retirement.

Maestas and Li (2007) consider what happens to workers who retire early because of burnout. They write that because burnout rises with continued exposure to stress at work, it should peak just prior to retirement then decline after the individual leaves the workplace. An individual for whom burnout is high enough to induce retirement may later unretire if she experiences boredom and believes that returning to work will outweigh any negative consequences of working. This notion of unretiring should help many older workers experiencing burnout to realize that the desire to work often returns in time and that retirement decisions based entirely on burnout may suggest that leaves of absence, requests for work assignment changes, and cycling over to other types of work may be alternatives. Keep in mind that it may be more difficult to return to work—at least to stimulating work—after you retire because breaks in a work record are often viewed in a negative light by employers.

An Example. Jack Briar is a 61-year-old upper-level manager of a large trucking company headquartered in the Midwest. He has been feeling burned out and unhappy about his job, believing that he is unappreciated and that politics led to the loss of a promotion that promised a better salary and greater work satisfaction. His feelings of burnout and unhappiness have been gaining in strength since Jack was passed over for a vice presidential position five years ago. Jack was one of the original managers of the company and has been instrumental in its growth and prosperity. He is now wondering if he should quit work completely or seek another job and has come for retirement counseling to help him decide on a course of action. Jack has no hobbies other than reading mysteries, watching films, and working. He wants the counselor to use a brief problem-solving approach that focuses on the present, doesn't assume that a problem has its origins in the past, and uses logical solutions.

The initial sessions went very well. Jack was highly motivated, did a great deal of reading about early retirement and older-adult burnout, and found that it wasn't unusual for people in his position to feel burned out and unhappy with their jobs after many years of tough, loyal, and successful work without very much financial or emotional payoff. As Jack read, talked to the counselor, and thought more about his job and the alternatives, he began to complain about feeling depressed. "I still don't know what to do," he said and wondered if the counselor had any suggestions. She did: why not enter the job market and see if he could find a job through which his skills could be put to better use and for which the salary and benefits were better?

Jack did just that, and much to his surprise, he was a finalist for several very high level positions in highly ranked companies. He spoke to the counselor about the experience. "I wanted something better, but now I'm scared. I don't think I want to work that hard, and I'm worried that having been in a smaller company makes me unprepared to deal with the high-level demands of a Fortune 500 corporation. The thought of moving makes me feel old and tired."

The counselor listened to Jack for several sessions as he discussed his confusion and concerns about his job possibilities. She told him that it seemed as if the pull to stay was stronger than the pull to leave. Was there a way he could stay at his current job and perhaps change what he was doing and begin to work less? Jack explored these options and came back with an idea:

I found out that we have an early retirement plan where you can get your pension and Social Security and still work for five years up to 50 percent of the time and get paid using your current salary and benefit level as a base. At the end of the five-year period, you can work part-time but at a lower salary rate. I think I could do that, and maybe it would help me deal with retirement. The problem is that I don't want to keep doing what I'm doing now, so I went to my boss and discussed the plan. He wants me to train new employees and to use some of the new in-service technology being developed by one of our consultants to improve productivity and safety, two issues we're having trouble with right now. He doesn't think we have enough diversity, and he wants to see a workforce that reflects the country better. He said that the reason I was passed over for the chair's position had nothing to do with me or other senior managers who wanted me, but the board wanted someone younger. It pissed me off to find out about ageism, but I had originally thought it was because they didn't like me. Having five years to ease myself into retirement would give me time to do some traveling. I live alone, and maybe it's time to find someone who can offer companionship and intimacy. I've put off those needs since I divorced 20 years ago, and I feel very lonely at times.

The counselor thought his idea was a good one and wondered how he might find someone to be in his life. "I was reading a mystery novel by the Swedish writer Henning Mankell called *Firewall* [New Press, 2002]," he said. "His main character, a cop called Kurt Wallander, is like me: lonely and set in his ways but in need of someone in his life. The detective uses a dating service and finds someone. I started thinking about women who have given me some indication that they are interested in me. Maybe I'll just follow up and see if I can find someone that way. I don't think I could ever use a dating service at my age, so we'll see. And I need to start going to our national conferences. I met my wife that way and we did pretty well for almost 20 years; not bad in this day and age."

GOOD AND BAD REASONS TO RETIRE

Good Reasons

1. You want to do something new with your life, and retirement will provide the free time and lack of other obligations to do it. A caveat, however: this assumes that you know what you want to do, have done the planning to

make it work, and have good reason to believe it will work before you retire.

2. You've missed out on family life, and now is the time to reengage with family; get to know your spouse, children, and grandchildren better; and learn about the joys of a strong extended family. I think you can do this while you're working as well, but if you have your mind set on it, be sure your family feels the same way.

Bad Reasons

1. You're burned out. This isn't a reason to retire; it's a reason to make some changes in your job responsibilities or career. There are a number of ways to deal with burnout, including new work assignments, changing jobs, and new careers. Once your burnout is over, what will you do with yourself if you've retired?

2. You're alone, and it's unlikely you'll meet anyone to be your mate, so work is the only way to occupy your time. Are you really trying to meet someone? Are you using strategies that have a good chance of working? Are you certain that there's nothing else to do other than work?

3. The stress of work is likely to compromise your health. This is a variation on being burned out. There are lots of ways to reduce stress and retiring isn't always one of them.

ADVICE ABOUT WHEN TO RETIRE

Only you know the best time to retire and the conditions that are most optimal for you, but the following suggestions may help:

1. You should keep on working until doing so is no longer an option. That means you've begun to lose your ability to work at a level acceptable to you and your employer and you can no longer keep your job. It helps if you can phase into retirement gradually. It also helps if you have a good idea that you'll be able to handle spare time and a schedule that doesn't include work to fill up your day. Extended vacations, leaves of absence, and part-time work before retirement can help you determine this. If you absolutely find free time hard to fill without work and leisure time isn't something you handle well, you need to begin thinking about a time when it may be difficult to continue working full-tilt and start practicing time management by developing outside interests. I know this may be difficult for some readers, but if you can put the same drive into finding outlets other than work that you put into your job, you'll develop some good ways of occupying your time with satisfying activities.

I play tennis three or four days a week. It's good for my health, it increases my energy to write, and it helps me meet new people. Many of the men and women with whom I play tennis are very high level people who had demanding jobs in business and industry and consider themselves hard workers and, when honest about it, workaholics. They all tell me that it takes time to fully accept retirement. Most of them continue to work part-time, and all say that gradually, they have accepted retirement and the leisure time that comes with it. All of them tell me that it's been a struggle and that no matter how much they plan, it takes time to accept retirement as a life condition. So just assume that there will be glitches here and there and like any major life change, it takes time to adjust.

2. If you have a date in mind when you're planning to retire, get as much information as possible about Medicare, your pension plans, Social Security, and your investments so you can anticipate if retirement will be financially feasible. I suggest that you start doing this at least two years before you plan to retire. Many people find the initial information about pension plans, Medicare, and Social Security a little hard to understand. The more time you have to plan your financial future, the better; you'll be able to decide if your time frame to retire is reasonable or if a little more time might be needed. That means making out a realistic budget and factoring in yearly cost-of-living increases. Don't lowball that estimate because you might find that you need more income once you've retired. Remember to figure in a reasonable cost-of-living increase (3% a year is the figure most financial advisors suggest) and medical cost-of-living increases, which are going up at the rate of 5 to 8 percent a year. It may help to read a book I wrote jointly with Brian Haas (Glicken & Hass, 2009) for the work Brian did to prepare people for financial issues before and during retirement.

3. This is especially important for those of you who have done little thinking about or planning for retirement. You should attend as many preretirement seminars as possible because each time you attend, you'll probably learn something new. You should also have serious discussions with your loved ones to make certain they support your decision, particularly your spouse if you're married. Being around someone a great deal more than either of you is used to can cause marital conflict. You might also talk to your retired friends and get their read on when to retire, although it's clearly a personal decision, and only you can decide when the time is right. I would include people who were ready to retire as well as those who weren't and, for certain, people you think of as having been work addicted.

4. In later chapters, I give some suggestions about ways to occupy your time, new careers, and new jobs, but for the time being, you should think seriously about everything related to the decision and then remember that most retired people go through stages and that one of the stages is regret. Many retired people retire and then unretire. One of my friends told me that it's absolutely true that you do regret leaving full-time work, but in time, when you get things settled in your life and have enough to keep you fully active, retirement is all about independence. It's a wonderful state to be in because you, not your job or anyone else, control your own destiny. The mix of leisure time, some work, family activities, volunteerism, travel, further education, and fulfilling your dreams can be intoxicating.

5. The decision to retire can be hard to make and the timing may not be completely right, but we're only human, and we can't know for sure how any decision will work out. That's why you'll need to have a fallback position if you find that retirement is not working for you. Agreements to let you

return to your job, new careers, and new work projects are all fallback positions, and you should take some time before you retire to develop them carefully.

In the following personal story, a 75-year-old woman talks about her life since retirement.

Personal Story: Life since Retirement

Retired is being tired twice, I've thought. First tired of working. Then tired of not.

"I've worked very hard all of my adult life, much of the time as a single mother supporting two daughters. I have a strong work ethic, and while I wouldn't call myself a workaholic, I'm certainly someone who's worked long and hard since I was a teenager. Many nights, when I'd come home from work, exhausted and tired of the turmoil and frustration involved in running a large medical practice in Long Beach, I'd dream of the day when I could retire. But when that day came 10 years ago, when I reached the age of 65 and started to collect Social Security, I had the chance to continue working. Going into the office three days a week was just enough to give me the best of both worlds. On one hand, I still enjoyed the camaraderie of my coworkers, and on the other hand, I had the time to volunteer and see how the rest of the world lived.

"Two years later, I decided to move to San Diego and was asked if I wanted to continue doing the same work, but strictly from home. I jumped at the chance. After six years in San Diego, I moved back to Long Beach, and my job came along with me, so I feel I'm still enjoying the best of both worlds.

"Since I've been semiretired, I've gone on a few trips. Hawaii is my favorite place to get away from it all. In my free time, I've read a mountain of books, done a barrel of crossword puzzles, called patrons for the San Diego Library System, volunteered at Jewish Family Service, a local hospice, and the Talbert Medical Group.

"I enjoy seeing movies in the afternoon (I've discovered that the audience at an afternoon showing of a good movie is usually made up of seniors). I also do my shopping when the stores are less crowded and the traffic lighter. I've learned to play the piano and attended classes in music appreciation, world affairs, and Singing for the Solo Voice. I've been on various boards, written a monthly newsletter for a singing group I belonged to, entered poetry contests, survived cancer and two knee replacements, and I can still leap over tall wastebaskets in a single stride.

"What I don't do is unnecessary housework, wash windows, prepare large meals, iron mountains of clothes, wear spike heels or plunging necklines, give up my spot on the recliner to someone younger, or try to impress everyone with my vast world knowledge and wardrobe of the stars. I no longer get a thrill out of proving to anyone that I was right, getting my children to see life my way, or trying to prove to people with opposing political views that I'm right and they're wrong.

"I can now honestly say that this isn't the retirement I had dreamed of. You know the one where you stay young and active with crowds of friends around you while you spend the tons of money you thought you were saving all those years of working so hard.

"I also know that I get bored more quickly than I thought I would, but I can honestly say that I don't miss the daily grind of being in an office 40 hours a week. Every time I visit the office and hear all the phones ringing at the same time and everyone looking a little harried, I know I don't miss that at all. I also don't miss the excuses people use to get their pain medication refills before their refills are due, although I must admit that some of them were very creative. I don't miss the traffic when daylight savings time changes and it's dark or raining, and I don't miss dealing with doctors, many of whom have God complexes. Some days I miss having someone in the next office to talk to and laugh with, but I soon get over that.

"I don't think retirement means the same to those of us who aren't part of a couple. Those of us who are single know that what we have to live on usually only comes from our own past earnings, and sometimes that makes life a little more tenuous. We usually hang on to what we have in terms of home and family and have already learned to be independent and creative. Probably the thing we most want to have at this stage of life is reasonably decent health and the energy to continue doing the things we enjoy.

"I've worked very hard all my life. I worked as a teenager and I still work hard, but I've taken a time-out from very hard work and given myself permission to enjoy life. I just had a 75th birthday celebration, and it was wonderful. My family and friends came, some from very far away. The food was great and the moment lives inside of me. My brother gave me a couple boxes of books to read. We're both mystery fans, and what he likes I seem to like as well. In the next month or two, I'll read everything he gave me.

"I'll relish the next time we get together as a family. I won't dwell on the people who once were friends but aren't any longer or the tough times I've had. Instead, I'll read this new batch of books, enjoy the work I still do, look forward to the next play or musical or opera I see with friends, and understand that you need to use your remaining time wisely. If you wait, there won't be any time left, and you'll only have the memories of hard work with little pleasure to take you into old age.

"Whatever life after retirement really means, for me it's the reality of living in the present. Retired life as you age has its ups and downs, but for the most part I'm content with the choices I've made and hope to keep making. I just want to be around for as many more years as I still have, with a clear head and laughter on my lips."—Gladys Smith, Long Beach, California.

SUMMARY

In this chapter, I discussed the many conflicting feelings and emotions that contribute to retirement anxiety and suggested ways of coping so that you can make the best decision possible. Even when that takes place, many retirees go through a short period of regret, which disappears as they become more comfortable with the many benefits of retired living. Retirement often provides opportunity for second careers and part-time work and much more leisure time to read, travel, become involved with community, and pursue personal interests and hobbies. The more planning you've done to develop a time to retire that is right for you, the more you will be able to transition to meaningful activities in retirement.

SUGGESTED WEB SITES

Do I really want to retire?, http://retireplan.about.com/od/caniretire/a/want_to_ retire.htm.

The relationship between job attitudes and the decision to retire, http://eric.ed.gov/ER ICDocs/data/ericdocs2sql/content_storage_01/0000019b/80/34/3d/2b. pdf.

Spousal influence on the decision to retire, http://www.economica.ca/ew02_1p3.htm.

When do you plan to retire?, http://www.community.wa.gov.au/DFC/Communi ties/Seniors/Retirement+Planning/Planning_an_Active_Retirement.htm.

REFERENCES

Atchley, R.C. (1975). Adjustment to the loss of job at retirement. *International Journal of Aging and Human Development, 6*, 17–27.

Atchley, R.C. (1982). Retirement: Learning the world of work. *Annals of the American Academy of Political and Social Sciences, 464*, 120–131.

Bossé, R., Aldwin, C.M., Levenson, M.R., & Workman-Daniels, K. (1991). How stressful is retirement? Findings from the Normative Aging Study. *Journals of Gerontology, 46*, 9–14.

Braithwaite, V.A., Gibson, D.M., & Bosly-Craft, R. (1986). An exploratory study of poor adjustment styles among retirees. *Social Science and Medicine, 23*, 493–499.

Fletcher, W.L., & Hansson, R.O. (1991). Assessing the social components of retirement anxiety. *Psychology and Aging, 6*, 76–85.

Glamser, F.D. (1976). Determinants of a positive attitude toward retirement. *Journals of Gerontology, 31*, 104–107.

Glicken, M.D., & Haas, B. (2009). *A simple guide to retirement: how to make retirement work for you*. Santa Barbara, CA: Praeger.

Isaksson, K. (1997). Patterns of adjustment to early retirement. *Reports from the Department of Psychology, 828*, 1–13.

Maestas, N., & Li, X. (2007, October). *Burnout and retirement decision*. Ann Arbor: Michigan Retirement Research Center, University of Michigan.

Martin-Matthews, A., & Brown, K.H. (1988). Retirement as a critical life event. *Research on Aging, 9,* 548–571.

Mor-Barak, M.E., & Tynan, M. (1993, January). Older workers and the workplace: A new challenge for occupational social work. *Social Work, 38,* 45–55.

Palmore, E.B., Fillenbaum, G.G., & George, L.K. (1984). Consequences of retirement. *Journal of Gerontology, 39,* 109–116.

Richardson, V.E., & Kilty, K.M. (1991). Adjustment to retirement: Continuity vs. discontinuity. *International Journal of Aging and Human Development, 33,* 151–169.

Sharpley, C.F., & Layton, R. (1998). Effects of age of retirement, reason for retirement and pre-retirement training on psychological and physical health during retirement. *Australian Psychologist, 33,* 119–124.

Walker, J., Kimmel, D., & Price, K. (1981). Retirement style and retirement satisfaction: Retirees aren't all alike. *International Journal of Clinical Psychology, 41,* 58–62.

PART IV

After Retirement: Repairing the Impact of Work Addiction on Physical and Mental Health

Chapters 9 through 12 discuss the important topics of your physical and mental health and what you can do to repair the stress and strain on your body and nervous system caused by too many years of overwork. Chapter 9 discusses loneliness after retirement and what you can do about it. Loneliness is often a key problem for work-addicted people after they retire. Chapter 10 discusses anxiety and depression. Chapter 11 discusses substance abuse, which is also a major problem for many workaholics before and after retirement. Chapter 12 discusses health issues and how to deal with some major problems related to aging after long careers at very stressful jobs.

CHAPTER 9

Loneliness

LONELINESS

Work-addicted people are particularly prone to feelings of loneliness in part because they've often failed to develop close relationships with others and lack relationship skills, and partly because when the heavy workload they've become accustomed to lessens, or in the case of unemployment tends to vanish, loneliness and depression sometimes set in.

Estimates of the prevalence of loneliness range from 7 to 84 percent in studies where older people are asked if they feel lonely (Sheldon, 1984; Wenger, 1983). Prince, Harwood, Blizard, and Thomas (1997) found that available studies of adults over age 65 indicate that 5 to 15 percent report frequently feeling lonely, and an additional 20 to 40 percent report occasional feelings of loneliness. However, 50 percent of adults aged 80 or over often feel lonely. Because of the tendency to give positive answers when the opposite may be true, we should interpret these findings cautiously and accept that rates of loneliness may be higher than those found in surveys.

Loneliness and Isolation   So that we're clear about the meaning of loneliness, here are a few definitions from the literature. Murphy (2006) describes *loneliness* "as a condition with distressing, depressing, dehumanizing, detached feelings that a person endures when there is a gaping emptiness in his or her life due to an unfulfilled social and/or emotional life" (p. 22). Uruk and Demir (2003) define *loneliness* as "an unpleasant experience that occurs when a person's network of social relationships is significantly deficient in either quality or quantity" (p. 179). The authors add that loneliness is "the psychological state that results from discrepancies between one's desire for and one's actual composition of relationships" (p. 179). Young (1982) defines *loneliness* as the "perceived absence of satisfying social relationships, accompanied by symptoms of psychological distress that are related to the perceived absence" (p. 380).

Uruk and Demir (2003) report a strong correlation between parents who have little time to spend with their children or fail to form attachments with their children and the development of loneliness in adolescence that often continues into adulthood and later life. Joiner, Catanzaro, Rudd, and Rajab (1999) believe that loneliness stems from a lack of pleasurable engagement and, as a result, a painful disconnection from trying to engage. Similarly, Jones and Carver (1991) believe that loneliness affects "one's opinion about people, life, and society in a manner suggesting that lonely people subscribe to negativistic, apathetical, and pessimistic views" (p. 400).

Weiss (1973) distinguishes loneliness due to emotional isolation from loneliness due to social isolation. Emotional isolation appears in the absence of a close emotional attachment (often related to a lack of parental attachment), while social isolation appears in the absence of an engaging social network (often related to a lack of peer support, friendships, and close social networks). Rubin and Mills (1991) believe that loneliness develops when a pattern made up of social anxiety, lack of dominance, and social isolation results in peer rejection and negative self-perception. Olweus (1993) reports that when children blame their own incompetence for negative social experiences with peers, which result in rejection, the end effect is often social withdrawal, feelings of isolation, and depression. Rotenberg, MacDonald, and King (2004) found considerable evidence that loneliness correlates highly with lack of trust, particularly in young women. The authors note that

the relationship between *loneliness* and trust is stronger for girls than it is for boys. The trust measures accounted for 57% of *loneliness* for girls but only 18% of *loneliness* for boys. These findings have implications for social functioning during adulthood. Women have larger intimacy networks than do men and, therefore, the observed association between *loneliness* and trust beliefs in same-gender peers may be stronger for women than for men during adulthood as well. (p. 235)

Aging and Loneliness   In explaining the reasons for loneliness and the large number of lonely older adults, Seligman and Csikszetmihalyi (2000) note that Americans "live surrounded by many more people than their ancestors did, yet they are intimate with fewer individuals and thus experience greater loneliness and alienation" (p. 9). Ostrov and Offer (1980) suggest that American culture emphasizes individual achievement, competitiveness, and impersonal social relations and that loneliness may be quite pronounced in the face of such socially alienating values. Saxton (1986) argues that in contemporary American society, there is a decline in the face-to-face, intimate contacts with family members, relatives, and close friends that were much more prevalent several decades ago. Mijuskovic (1992) views American society as highly mechanized with "impersonal institutions, disintegration of the family as a result of a high divorce rate, [and a] high mobility rate with its impact on family and community ties; the fast-paced living and self-centeredness of the culture interferes with people's ability to establish and maintain fulfilling relationships" (Rokach, 2007, p. 184).

Many lonely people report feeling lonely and rejected by others from a very early age and even in the presence of others. Among lonely older people who have experienced loneliness from an early age, the absence of social contacts as they age creates a sense of despair that should not be confused with depression. The loneliness they experience is a feeling of separateness and not fitting in that sometimes worsens with age. This type of loneliness may have its roots in a failure to bond with parents or parental rejection. A case at the end of the chapter describes the treatment for this type of loneliness.

Loneliness Affects Health Lonely people tend to have more anger problems than nonlonely people, eat foods that are higher in sugar and fat content, and as a result, often suffer from high blood pressure and other cardiovascular problems including stroke and heart disease. They also have more immune deficiency problems, experience less restful sleep, and suffer from cognitive decline as they age.

Russell (1996) found a relationship between loneliness, chronic illness, and lower self-rated health status in older adults. McWhiter (1990) found links between loneliness and suicide and suicidal thoughts. Older adult loneliness has been found to increase alcohol abuse (Akerlind & Hornquist, 1992) and depression (Russell, 1996). Copel (1988) suggests that loneliness can reduce a sense of self-worth and inhibit the ability to develop and maintain interpersonal relationships. Peters and Liefbroer (1997) found that older adults not involved in a partner relationship were lonelier than older adults with a partner and that the loss or lack of a partner affected males more than females. Men rely on their spouses for social support, suggesting the absence of a strong social network when compared to women. Dependence on a spouse for support and companionship can lead to extreme loneliness when the spouse dies and prolonging bereavement. As a result, widowed men tend to remarry at a much higher rate than widowed women. Martikainen and Valkonen (1996) found that the death of a spouse affects everyday tasks such as housecleaning, preparing food, and taking needed medication. Anderson and Diamond (1995) found that older widowed men experience difficulties in everyday tasks such as cooking and meal planning. Many of the men in this study who thought they were good cooks found it difficult to cook or even to plan a meal.

The *Brown University Long-Term Care Quality Advisor* ("Loneliness May Predict," 1998) reports that elderly individuals who indicate a high degree of loneliness tend to be admitted to nursing homes sooner than those who are not so lonely.

Bennett (1980) reports that social isolation among older adults has long been recognized as a problem that diminishes their well-being because of its association with problems of low morale, poor health, and the risk of premature institutionalization. Sorkin, Roo, and Lu (2002) found that social isolation and loneliness compromise immune function and have been linked to cardiovascular disease. Additionally, lonely people are more likely to suffer from cardiovascular disease because their lifestyles may include little or no exercise, unhealthy eating habits, alcohol abuse, and the lack of a support network. Feeling love and support from others helps encourage lonely older adults to maintain physical health (Blazer, 2002b).

Blazer (2002a) reports that loneliness may be a risk factor for the low-level depression that continues to be a leading mental health problem for older adults. Cohen (2000) suggests that loneliness in later life may be thought of as a "near-depression" and advises mental health professionals to reconsider the research and interventions used to treat loneliness.

The Internet as a Way of Coping with Loneliness   The use of the Internet has dramatically increased in older adults. Kadlec (2007) reports that in adults over the age of 50, 54 percent use the Internet and 24 percent have high-speed hookups. That's up sharply from 38 and 5 percent in 2002, respectively. Almost all older adults who go online (87%) use e-mail, although there is a big dropoff at present in adults over the age of 70. Kadlec reports that retired people are online an average of nine hours a week and that the amount of time they spend on the Internet will increase as computer-savvy adults age.

White and colleagues (2002) believe that the Internet and more specifically e-mail has the potential to increase social support and the emotional well-being of older adults in the following ways: they can use computers to communicate often, cheaply, and easily with family, friends, and others who have computers; they can get information about a variety of issues, particularly health and financial issues; they can explore hobbies and learn information about their community; and they can meet new people and broaden their support systems through chat rooms and bulletin boards. The authors write that "in essence, relatively isolated and disabled older adults can reconnect, strengthen and broaden their connection with the outside world by incorporating computer technology into their lives" (p. 214).

In a study done by White and colleagues (2002) to teach lonely frail older adults with a mean age of 71 to use the Internet, the authors report that 60 percent of the total sample and 74 percent of those who completed the nine-hour training course were using the Internet weekly within five months. Because of problems with the testing instruments used, a statistically significant relationship between using the Internet and a decrease in feelings of loneliness was not found. However, the authors write that "looking only at the intervention group and comparing users to non-users there were trends toward decreased loneliness and depression" (p. 219). In summary, the authors note that

the Internet is an exciting new technology with much potential for enriching the lives of many older adults. As a source of information, social activity, and interpersonal communication, the Internet may expand the constrained boundaries of congregate housing, retirement communities, and even skilled care nursing facilities. Depending on the older user, this expansion may include more frequent contacts with family and friends, new opportunities to pursue former interests, as well as avenues to meet new friends and to "travel" to places no longer accessible due to health limitations. (p. 220)

TREATING LONELINESS AND ISOLATION: A CASE EXAMPLE

What happens when older adult workaholics who have been successful in many aspects of their lives are unable to shake severe feelings of loneliness when they retire? The following case study deals with that issue and begins with a 70-year-old male discussing lifelong feelings of loneliness and how he's coping with those feelings following retirement. Thanks to SAGE Publications for permission to reprint this case, which was first printed in Glicken (2006). (Excerpted from Glicken, M.D. *Learning from resilient people: Lessons we can apply to counseling and psychotherapy.* Thousand Oaks, CA: SAGE Publications, 2006. Pp. 176–178. Reprinted with permission.)

Dr. Jacob Goldstein is a divorced 70-year-old former English professor who has just retired to a community of scholars and researchers built by a large research university in the Southwest to help retired university faculty and administrators continue their scholarly work and to have social and professional contacts with other scholars. He is a classic workaholic who has few interests outside his field of interest and has always had trouble connecting with people outside of work. Before he retired, he worked 12 to 14 hours a day during the workweek and often as much as 6 to 8 hours a day during weekends and vacations. He lacks hobbies and other interests and says that he's burned out on academic work but has little else to occupy his time.

Dr. Goldstein chose the academic retirement community because he thought the university affiliation would make the people similar to those he'd worked with all of his life. He spoke to me about what he describes as lifelong loneliness and how he is coping with it in retirement. He told me, "I think people who grow up in very troubled families never quite get the hang of intimate relationships. In my family, we were so busy surviving poverty and the illness of my mother that none of us really mastered the ability to be loved or to love someone in return. My father's favorite saying was that it was better to be home by yourself reading a good book than to be out with bad friends. Of course, he considered all my friends to be bad, so I spent my childhood reading books, pretty much alone.

"People sometimes think I'm arrogant because I'm so standoffish, but I'm really very shy and introverted. I don't think people react well to me. I'm never invited to dinner by colleagues, or asked out for coffee, or any of the things that tell me others find me appealing. Sometimes it's very hurtful.

Even so, I've been quite successful at work and I've written several well-received scholarly books and several less well received novels and books of poetry before retiring from an Ivy League college as a full professor. Before I retired, and even now, I experience loneliness when I'm not working on books. It can be a killer. I've tried everything, including going to as many social functions as possible, to fill my time, but I feel even more alone and isolated when I'm with people I don't know. It's hard to explain being lonely when you're around people.

"I've gone for therapy, of course, but most of the time it's so superficial and completely misses the mark that it ends up hurting me more than helping. You go to a therapist and it's like falling in love. You have high expectations and when they're not met and you've put in so much time and energy to get another person to listen, to maybe even *like* you a little and they don't, it hurts.

"My marriage was a disaster. My ex-wife thought I was married to my job, and very early on we both felt emotionally divorced. I've had some brief relationships, but they always end with a certain amount of rancor on the part of the women I've dated. They all find me withdrawn and unable to give them the emotional warmth they expect.

"For years, whenever I felt really lonely, I'd just automatically put time into my work. It didn't give me a lot of pleasure, except for a couple things I did on loneliness. After a while it just became a habit. If I felt lonely or if I had time to kill, I'd work.

"I fight feeling down all the time. I force myself to get up in the morning and write or go to coffee at the community center where there are some guys like me who are single and want to kibitz a bit. I don't find it satisfying, and I haven't made any friends since I've been here. I joined the tennis club, but I play with people who don't seem to want to develop a friendship with me. Because of the heat for much of the year, we play at 6:00 A.M., and when we're done, I go home to my empty condo. My lady friend, another university professor, comes over at night after work, but I feel lonely with her as well. We haven't much to say, so we watch TV in silence. I always experience a feeling of mild despair. I wouldn't call it a depression, but it's always there.

"I'm seeing a therapist now to help me with the adjustment to not working. It's helping, I think. She's been working on the origins of my loneliness, and I'm astonished at how powerful it is to review the events in my life through fresh eyes. Knowing more about myself now, I've come to believe that I have to fight the urge to give up and that I have to keep trying my best. My therapist has done a good job of getting me to continue going to social events, even though I feel like giving up. I have to admit it's paying off some. I have a tendency to assume that other people I don't know don't like me when, perhaps, I'm distancing myself from them. So I practice not doing that. It's helping me have social contacts I would not have been patient enough to develop before I went into therapy. My therapist has urged me to read about loneliness and to join chat rooms with other lonely people. It's an eye-opener to find out that other people feel the same way I do, many of them even more successful than me.

"My therapist also urged me to join a self-help group. At first I thought it was a dumb idea. All I could think was that it would be like AA: 'Hi, my name is Jake and I'm lonely.' It wasn't like that at all. I've met some very nice people. We go to concerts and movies together. A few of the men and I meet for dinner once a week, and after talking about loneliness, we started talking about us. It was amazing to find such nice but hurting people. I've never really had a good and true friend, but the guys feel that way to me. Who would have guessed?

"My therapist is a very gentle person, but under the gentleness she's firm and direct. I was very touched to find out that she read one of my novels. We talked about it and used it in therapy because there were many themes of isolation and loneliness in the book. She had perceptions of it I didn't even have. I've always had a low opinion of therapy until this experience, and now I think it's just great because we have this equal relationship and she really wants to hear what I think. I've been an educator all my life, and what she's doing sort of feels like very sophisticated mentoring. I don't even know what kind of therapist she is, she's just awfully good.

"I don't think there's an easy answer to loneliness other than to keep on working at it. You keep on trying, you don't allow yourself to feel too sorry for yourself, and you take each day as it comes. I know those are clichés, but sometimes there is truth in a cliché."

Discussion with the Therapist

Dr. Goldstein's therapist told me the following: "People who have lifelong problems with loneliness have a bit of paranoia about other people. They expect the worst, and when it happens, they're not surprised. When he called for an appointment and told me he was having trouble fitting in with others in the retirement community, I did a lot of reading about retirement and loneliness. I also tried to imagine how difficult it would be to retire after a long work life, a work addiction, feelings of isolation, and then to come somewhere and resettle all by myself. That takes a lot of energy and positive thinking. I also read one of Dr. Goldstein's novels. It was a wonderful novel about lonely people. It told me a lot about him. I mentioned I'd read his novel, and he was thrilled. He wanted to know if it told me anything about him. I told him it did, and the discussion was really a breakthrough.

"After talking about his novel, he was much more open to the suggestions I made and worked very hard at dealing with shyness and a sense that others don't like him. It's tough work because it's almost a habit for him to think that social events will end badly and that people won't like him. He was the professor of the year for three years at a very prestigious university, and yet he thinks others don't like him and avoid him. He's begun to see the signals he gives others to stay away, and they, of course, do. Now he's giving off more positive messages, and much to his amazement, people are reaching out to him. Intimacy is still a problem. His relationship with his lady friend feels very rigid and unemotional. He doesn't like it, and they've begun to talk about coming for couple's therapy.

"All in all, I think he's a very lonely and isolated man, but he's trying, and the results are paying off. Will they continue? I think they will. I plan on doing a lot of follow-up after he leaves treatment. Lonely people have spent many years practicing being lonely. In some ways, it's satisfying to retreat inside their homes rather than face social challenges. But we live in hope, and I have a good sense that Dr. Goldstein will handle this challenge much as he's handled others: with inner resolve, dignity, and great effort."

SUMMARY

This chapter provided reasons for social isolation and loneliness, which sometimes leads to depression in older adults. Internal and external reasons for loneliness were explored, and a case study was presented of a lonely older man and the counseling he received for loneliness, and why it seemed to help him. A later chapter will explore the issue of counseling for work addictions.

REFERENCES

Akerlind, I., & Hornquist, J. (1992). Loneliness and alcohol abuse: A review of evidence of an interplay. *Social Science and Medicine, 34*, 405–414.

Anderson, K., & Diamond, M. (1995). The experience of bereavement in older adults. *Journal of Advanced Nursing, 22*, 308–315.

Bennett, R. (1980). *Aging, isolation, and resocialization.* New York: VanNostrand Reinhold.

Blazer, D. G. (2002a). *Depression in late life* (3rd ed.). New York: Springer.

Blazer, D. G. (2002b). Self-efficacy and depression in late life: A primary prevention proposal. *Aging and Mental Health, 6*, 315–324.

Burke, M. (2009, August 24). John T. Cacioppo: Loneliness can kill you. *Forbes, 184*(3), 22–23.

Cohen, G. D. (2000). Loneliness in later life. *American Journal of Geriatric Psychiatry, 8*, 273–275.

Copel, L. C. (1988). Loneliness. *Journal of Psychosocial Nursing, 26*(1), 14–19.

Glicken, M. D. (2006). *Learning from resilient people: Lessons we can apply to counseling and psychotherapy.* Thousand Oaks, CA: Sage.

Joiner, T. E., Jr., Catanzaro, S., Rudd, M. D., & Rajab, M. H. (1999). The case for a hierarchical, oblique, and bidimensional structure of loneliness. *Journal of Social and Clinical Psychology, 18*, 47–75.

Jones, W., & Carver, M. (1991). Adjustment and coping implications of loneliness. In C.R. Snyder (Ed.), *Handbook of social and clinical psychology* (pp. 67–93). New York: Pergamon Press.

Kadlec, D. (2007, February 12). Senior netizens. *Time, 169*(7), 94.

Loneliness may predict nursing home admission. (1998, May). *Brown University Long-Term Care Quality Advisor, 10*(5), 3.

Martikainen, P., & Valkonen, T. (1996). Mortality after the death of a spouse: Rates and causes of death in a large Finnish cohort. *American Journal of Public Health, 86*, 1087–1093.

McWhiter, B. (1990). Loneliness: A review of current literature, with implications for counselling and research. *Journal of Counselling and Development, 68*, 417–422.

Mijuskovic, B. (1992). Organic communities, atomistic societies and loneliness. *Journal of Sociology and Social Welfare, 19*, 147–164.

Murphy, F. (2006). Loneliness: A challenge for nurses caring for older people. *Nursing Older People, 18*(5), 22–25.

Olweus, D. (1993). Victimization by peers: Antecedents and long-term outcomes. In K.H. Rubin & J.B. Asendorpf (Eds.), *Social withdrawal, inhibition and shyness in childhood* (pp. 315–341). Hillsdale, NJ: Lawrence Erlbaum Associates.

Ostrov, E., & Offer, D. (1980). Loneliness and the adolescent. In J. Hartog, J.R. Audy, & Y. Cohen (Eds.), *The anatomy of loneliness* (pp. 170–185). New York: International University Press.

Peters, A., & Liefbroer, A.C. (1997). Beyond marital status: Partner history and well-being in old age. *Journal of Marriage and the Family, 59*, 687–699.

Prince, M.J., Harwood, R.H., Blizard, R.A., & Thomas, A. (1997). Social support deficits, loneliness and life events as risk factors for depression in old age: The Gospel Oak Project VI. *Psychological Medicine, 27*, 323–332.

Rokach, A. (2007). The effect of age and culture on the causes of loneliness. *Social Behavior and Personality, 35*, 169–186.

Rotenberg, K.J., MacDonald, K.J., & King, E.V. (2004). The relationship between loneliness and interpersonal trust during middle childhood. *Journal of Genetic Psychology, 165*, 233–249.

Rubin, K.H., & Mills, R.S.L. (1991). Conceptualizing developmental pathways to internalizing disorders in childhood. *Canadian Journal of Behavioral Science, 23*, 300–317.

Russell, D. (1996). ULCA Loneliness Scale (version 3): Reliability, validity, and factor structure. *Journal of Personality Assessment, 66*, 20–40.

Saxton, L. (1986). *The individual, marriage and family*. Belmont, CA: Wadsworth.

Seligman, M.E.P., & Csikszetmihalyi, M. (2000). Positive psychology: An introduction. *American Psychologist, 55*, 5–14.

Sheldon, J. (1984). *The social medicine of old age: A report of an enquiry in Wolverhampton*. Milton Keynes, UK: Open University Press.

Sorkin, D., Rook, K.S., & Lu, J.L. (2002). Loneliness, lack of emotional support, lack of companionship, and the likelihood of having a heart condition in an elderly sample. *Annals of Behavioral Medicine, 24*, 290–298.

Uruk, A.C., & Demir, A. (2003). Loneliness. *Journal of Psychology, 137*, 179–194.

Weiss, R.S. (1973). *Loneliness: The experience of emotional and social isolation*. Cambridge, MA: MIT Press.

Wenger, G. (1983). Loneliness: A problem of measurement. In D. Jerome (Ed.), *Ageing in modern society* (pp. 163–218). London: Croom Helm.

White, H., McConnell, E., Clipp, E., Branch, L. G., Sloane, R., Pieper, C., et al. (2002). A randomized controlled trial of the psychosocial impact of providing Internet training and access to older adults. *Aging and Mental Health, 6*(3), 213–221.

Young, J.E. (1982). Loneliness, depression, and cognitive therapy: Theory and applications. In L.A. Peplau & D. Perlman (Eds.), *Loneliness: A sourcebook of current theory, research and therapy* (pp. 379–405). New York: John Wiley.

CHAPTER 10

Anxiety and Depression

ANXIETY

Large numbers of anxious older adults often go undiagnosed and untreated because underlying symptoms of anxiety are thought to be physical in nature, and professionals frequently believe that older adults are neither motivated for therapy nor find it an appropriate treatment. This often leaves many older adults trying to cope with serious emotional problems without adequate help. As this chapter will report, the number of older adults dealing with anxiety is considerable and growing as the number of older adults increases in America. Health problems, loss of loved ones, financial insecurities, lack of a support group, and a growing sense of isolation and lack of worth are common problems among the elderly that lead to serious symptoms of anxiety and depression, problems that often coexist among many older adults.

The prevalence of anxiety disorders has usually been thought to decrease with age, but recent findings suggest that generalized anxiety is actually a more common problem among the elderly than depression. A study reported by Beekman et al. (1998) found anxiety to affect 7.3 percent of an elderly population as compared to 2 percent for depression in the same population. Lang and Stein (2001) estimate that the percentage of older Americans suffering from anxiety could be in excess of 10 percent and could be as high as 18 percent, making anxiety the most common psychiatric symptom for older adults (Lang & Stein, 2001). Anxiety and depression among older adults frequently exist together with typical physical indications including chest pains, heart palpitations, night sweats, shortness of breath, essential hypertension, headaches, and generalized pain. Because physicians often fail to diagnose underlying symptoms of anxiety and depression in elderly patients, the emotional component of the symptoms is frequently not dealt with. Definitions and descriptions of anxiety used to diagnosis younger patients often fail to capture the unique stressors that older adults must deal with or the fragile nature of life for older adults as they attempt to cope with limited finances, failing health, the deaths of loved ones, concerns about their own mortality, and a sense of uselessness and hopelessness because their roles as adults have been dramatically altered with age and retirement.

Lang and Stein (2001) found that women have higher rates of anxiety across all age groups and that older adults who have had anxiety problems in the past are more at risk of the problem worsening as they age. Agoraphobia (the fear of leaving one's home) may also be more likely to have late-life onset as a result of physical limitations, disabilities, unsafe neighborhoods, and other factors that make some older adults fearful of leaving home. Because anxiety in the elderly may have a physical base or may realistically be connected to concerns about health, Kogan, Edelstein, and McKee (2000) provide some guidelines for distinguishing an anxiety disorder in the elderly from anxiety related to physical problems.

A physical cause of anxiety is more likely if the onset of anxiety comes suddenly, the symptoms fluctuate in strength and duration, and fatigue has been present before the symptoms of anxiety were felt. The authors identify the following medical problems as reasons for symptoms of anxiety: (1) medical problems that include endocrine, cardiovascular, pulmonary, or neurological disorders and (2) the impact of certain medications, most notably stimulants, beta-blockers, certain tranquilizers, and of course, alcohol.

An emotional cause of anxiety is more likely if the symptoms have lasted two or more years with little change in severity and if the person has coexisting emotional symptoms. However, anxiety may cycle on and off or a lower level of generalized anxiety may be present that causes the elderly client a great deal of discomfort. Obsessive concerns about financial issues and health are common and realistic worries that trouble elderly clients. The concerns may be situational or constant but not serious enough to lead to a diagnosis of anxiety; nonetheless, they cause the client unhappiness and may actually lead to physical problems, including high blood pressure, cardiovascular problems, sleep disorders, and an increased use of alcohol and over-the-counter medications to lessen symptoms of anxiety.

Pingitore and Sansone (1998) suggest the following steps to determine if you or a loved one have an anxiety disorder:

1. Consider the possibility of a medical problem as the cause of the older adult's anxiety-related symptoms.

2. If this is not the case, consider the possibility of substance use or drug inter-actions in the client's anxiety.

3. If this is not the case, determine if the symptoms are better explained by another emotional problem such as depression, loneliness, unemployment, or a life crisis common to early retirement issues.

Treatment of Anxiety Problems   Beck and Stanley (1997) and Stanley and Novy (2000) report positive results with anxious older clients using cognitive-behavioral therapy and relaxation training. Benefits for older clients experiencing anxiety appear to be as positive as they are with youn-ger clients. Smith, Sherrill, and Celenda (1995) have found that older adults respond well to psychotherapy for anxiety, "especially if it supports their religious beliefs and encourages life review that helps to resolve both hid-den and obvious conflicts associated with specific events in the patient's life history" (p. 6). The authors recommend medications only after all op-tions have been considered. Most anxiety problems in younger clients are treated with benzodiazepines, but these have only a "marginal efficacy for chronic anxiety and are especially bad for older adults because the body accumulates the drug and may produce excess sedation, diminished sex-ual desire, worsening of dementing illness, and a reduction in the gen-eral level of energy" (Smith et al., 1995, p. 6). The authors also warn that Prozac may actually cause anxiety as a side effect and recommend pin-pointing the cause of the anxiety problem before considering the use of medications.

Lang and Stein (2001) recommend that treatment of anxiety in older adults should be tailored to the individual needs and cognitive abilities of the person. Some older clients resent advice given by professionals younger than they are. They may find relaxation approaches inappropriate or child-ish. And they may view changes in the way they are told to perceive life events as dangerous to their survival because long-held beliefs and behav-iors have often served them well in the past. Being asked to view a situation with clarity and rationality may suggest to the older adult that counselors believe they are lying about an event. Older work addicted adults may discount psychological explanations for their anxiety and prefer to think that it has a physical origin.

A helpful suggestion is to provide reading materials to help anxious older adults understand the origins of their anxiety and the approach most likely to help relieve their symptoms. Testimonials from other workaholics who have successfully been helped might also be helpful. Keep in mind that older work addicted adults may be suffering, but they also fear that accepting new ways of approaching life may actually increase their level of anxiety. However, as Lang and Stein (2001) report, there are harmful side effects to the long-term use of many antianxiety medications. Though some of the counseling approaches used in the treatment of anxiety may not always fit an older workaholic adult's frame of reference, it's wise to let them know about medical treatments and the potential for harm as one way to acknowledge that medications have risks that should be considered, just as there are associated risks in doing nothing.

Personal Story: Social Anxiety

"I'm 64 and I've been anxious in social situations for as long as I can remember. I don't feel anxiety in my work life, but when it comes to meeting people at parties I feel like that famous story of William Faulkner at a party in Hollywood. He was so uncomfortable that he kept backing up toward the balcony of the home where the party was being held until he fell over the balcony and landed in the swimming pool. That's the way I feel at parties. It's agony. I avoid parties or social activities where I don't know people, and even if I *do* know them, I assume they'll ignore me or avoid me, which is even worse.

"Because I feel so lonely and anxious when I'm with people, I've put much of my energy into work. I spend weekends working when I'd rather be doing something with friends or someone I love, but my anxiety about people makes that really tough. I should have retired two years ago but I keep working because it gives me something to do. The truth is that I feel very burned out, and I daydream about traveling and seeing new places but the thought of doing it alone stops me cold. I know I'd feel very odd about myself, and I obsess that I'd spend all the time traveling in some room by myself.

"My brother and sister both feel the same way, so I have to guess that it had a lot to do with our upbringing. My parents didn't want us socializing with other kids because they thought they'd be a bad influence on us. I think we all felt like outsiders. Even as a kid I didn't think people liked me much, and I still feel that way. One of my friends says that maybe I put up a shield that tells people to lay off. It might be true, but whatever I do, the end result is that social events are agony and I feel awful about myself when I go, and just as awful when I decide to avoid them.

"Maybe I'm an anxious person to begin with. I worry a lot, and I always seem to think the worst is going to happen. For a couple of years in my mid-40s I was on medication for generalized anxiety that was so bad I went into therapy. It didn't help much, and neither did the medication. Gradually, as I divorced and eliminated many of my responsibilities, I became a lot less anxious. I sleep well now and I'm productive, but up until my early 50s, I guess you could say I was pretty anxious.

"I also notice that I obsess about people and the slights they've done to me. I feel absolute blinding hatred for anyone who's critical of me. If I play sports and someone says something mean or obnoxious about the way I play, or look, or the clothes I wear, I think about it for weeks. It's all I can do not to wrap my racket around their heads. Who knows where this hostility comes from? I don't, and I've been in enough therapy that I should know by now.

"I've concluded that life isn't a bowl of cherries and that Forrest Gump was wrong. It's tough, and you have to hang on tight or you'll just fly off into space and never be seen again. I guess I feel that way a lot, that I'm invisible and that when I die, no one will even remember me. I don't know, you work hard, you try your best, you do the things no one else can do, and still you end up feeling unloved and unwanted. It's like a knife in your heart where your feelings live. The anxiety mystifies me. What am I anxious about? I don't know. Maybe magically something will happen and I won't care about other people. Maybe I'll get it right when I'm 70. Two years to go. It can't happen soon enough."—RJS

DEPRESSION

In a study of older adults living in a specific community, Blazer, Hughes, and George (1987) found that 8 percent had symptoms of depression or other disorders serious enough to warrant treatment. Wallis (2000) reports a depression rate of 6 percent among older adults, nearly two-thirds of whom are women. Wallis notes that depression is more prevalent among an older population because of loss of loved ones, health problems, and the inability to live independently. Mills and Henretta (2001) indicate that more than 2 million of the 34 million older Americans suffer from some form of depression, yet late-life depression is often undiagnosed or underdiagnosed.

Casey (1994) reports on a study that found that rates of suicide among adults 65 and older were almost double compared to the general population and that the completion rate for suicide among older adults was 1 in 4, as compared to 1 in 100 for the general population (Casey, 1994), suggesting that older adults are much more likely to see suicide as a final solution rather than a cry for help. Older adults who commit suicide often suffer from major depression, alcoholism, severe medical problems, and social isolation (Casey, 1994). Although adults aged 65 and older comprise only 13 percent of the U.S. population, they accounted for 18 percent of the total number of suicides that occurred in 2000. The highest rate of suicide (19.4 per 1,000) was among people aged 85 and over, a figure that is twice the overall national rate. The second highest rate (17.7 per 100,000) is among adults aged 75 to 84.

The Symptoms of Depression   Though symptoms of depression are consistent across age groups, Wallis (2000) suggests that older adults may express depression through such physical complaints as insomnia, eating disorders, and digestive problems. They may also show signs of lethargy, have less incentive to participate in the activities they enjoyed before they became depressed, and experience symptoms of depression while denying that they are depressed. Mild and transient depression brought on by situational events usually resolve themselves in time, but moderate depression may interfere with daily life activities and can result in social withdrawal and isolation. Severe depression may result in psychotic-like symptoms, including hallucinations and a loss of being in touch with reality (Wallis, 2000).

Zalaquett and Stens (2006) believe that depression is often undiagnosed and untreated in older adults, causing "needless suffering for the family and for the individual who could otherwise live a fruitful life" (p. 192). The authors point out that we have sufficient evidence that long-standing depression predicts earlier death, while recovery leads to prolonged life. Suicide is a significant risk factor for older adult clients suffering from depression. Depression, according to the authors, may increase the risk of physical illnesses and disability. Unützer et al. (2001) report that depression affects between 5 and 10 percent of older adults who visit a primary care provider and is a chronic, recurrent problem affecting many older adults, especially those with poor physical health. The authors note that late-life depression has been associated with substantial "individual suffering, functional impairment, losses in health-related quality of life, poor adherence to medical treatments and increased mortality from suicide and medical illnesses" (p. 505).

Hepner et al. (2007) found that primary care physicians do well in detecting and initiating treatment for depression but provide substantially "lower-quality care in terms of completion of a minimal course of treatment for depression (especially among elderly persons) or assessment and treatment of psychiatric co-morbid conditions" (p. 324). In addition, the researchers found little evidence of appropriate responses to suicidal ideations, low rates of referral to mental health specialists for complex patients, and low rates of completion of treatment, even though 85 percent of the patients were open to treatment.

Older adults also have a considerably higher suicide completion rate than other groups. Whereas for all age groups combined, there is one completed suicide ending in death for every 20 attempts, there is one completed suicide ending in death for every 4 attempts among adults who are 65 and older (Older Women's League, 2004). The National Center for Injury Prevention and Control (2005) reports that 14.3 of every 100,000 people aged 65 and older died by suicide in 2004, higher than the rate of about 11 per 100,000 in the general population. Non-Hispanic white men aged 85 and older were most likely to die by suicide, with an astonishing rate of 49.8 suicide deaths per 100,000 persons in that age group.

Reasons for Older Adult Depression   Although socioeconomic status has often been thought to predict life span and overall health, Robert and Li (2001) found evidence of a relationship between levels of community health and individual health. Lawton (1977) believes that older adults experience the community as their primary source of support, recreation, and stimulation rather than family or a core of friends. Lawton and Nahemow (1973) suggest that healthy community environments are particularly important for older adults who may have emotional, physical, or cognitive problems. Robert and Li (2001) define healthy communities as having a physical environment with limited noise, manageable traffic, and adequate lighting; a social environment with low crime rates, safe environments to walk in, and easy access to shopping; and a service environment that includes easy and safe access to inexpensive transportation, senior centers, medical care, and meal sites.

Social support networks for older adults are also a factor in positive physical and mental health. Tyler and Hoyt (2000) studied the emotional impact of natural disasters on older adults who had predisaster indications of depression and found that subjects with consistent social supports had lower levels of depression before and after a natural disaster than depressed subjects without social supports. In a study of successful aging, Vaillant and Mukamal (2001) found that one can predict longer and healthier lives before the age of 50 by considering the following indicators: family cohesion, preexisting major depression, ancestral longevity, childhood temperament, and physical health at age 50. Negative behaviors affecting physical and emotional health over which one has control include alcohol abuse, smoking, marital instability, lack of exercise, obesity, unsuccessful coping mechanisms, and lower levels of education.

In describing why many older people have been symptom-free and indeed are considered to be resilient in the face of serious trauma, Kramer (2005) believes that resilience may move into depression many years after a successfully coped with trauma. "Depression," he writes, "is not universal even in terrible times. Though prone to mood disorders, the great Italian writer Primo Levi, who committed suicide at the height of his success at age 67, was not depressed in his months at Auschwitz" (p. 53). Kramer continues,

I have treated a handful of patients who survived horrors arising from war or political repression. They come to depression years after enduring extreme privation. Typically such a person will say: "I don't understand it. I went through——," and here he will name a shameful event of our time. "I lived through *that* and in those months, I never felt *this.*" *This* refers to the relentless bleakness of depression, the self as hollow shell. Beset by great evil, a person can be wise, observant and disillusioned and yet not be depressed. Resilience confers its own measure of insight. (p. 53)

Not surprisingly, Mavandadi, Sorkin, Rook, and Newsom (2007) found a strong relationship between negative social interactions with older adults and physical pain and depression. The authors note that "negative exchanges with social network members may be sources of acute stress or chronic strain that could detract considerably from psychological well-being" (p. 815). Negative exchanges might include sending messages that convey displeasure and criticism, blaming the older adult for his pain and depression, making suggestions that appear critical and unlikely to help the older adult, and a lack of concern about the pain the older adult is in. The researchers urge treatment personnel to be aware of the relationship between pain, negative social interactions, and depression and report that when social interactions improve as a result of treatment, pain and depression subside.

Treating Depression in Older People Gallagher-Thompson, Hanley-Peterson, and Thompson (1990) followed elderly clients for two years after completion of treatment and found that 52 to 70 percent of the clients receiving three different types of often-used counseling had no return of depressed symptoms two years after treatment. The authors report that these rates of improvement are consistent with a younger population of depressed clients. Lebowitz and colleagues (1997) found that combining counseling that uses understanding past events in a person's life with antidepressant medication appeared to provide the most benefit. The authors note that about 80 percent of older adults with depression recovered with this kind of combined treatment and had lower recurrence rates than with psychotherapy or medication alone.

Zalaquett and Stens (2006) believe we have "a great body of data supporting the use of medication and/or psychosocial therapy to help the person with [late-life] depression return to a happier, more fulfilling life . . . and shorten the time to recovery" (p. 192). The National Institutes of Health (NIH Consensus Panel on Diagnosis and Treatment of Depression in Late Life, 1992) found that there are many different treatments for depression in older adults that have been shown to be safe and effective. Roth and Fonagy (1996) report that group therapies with older adults experiencing depression showed promise in reducing symptoms of depression. In summarizing treatment effectiveness with older clients experiencing depression, Myers and Harper (2004) report that many interventions have been found to be effective with older adults.

Personal Story: A Workaholic Seeks Help for Depression

"I went for counseling when my second marriage began to go bad. My wife said that I loved my job more than her. She may have been right. I was never home, and while I didn't love my job, maybe I didn't love her either. It began to occur to me that working 80 hours a week left me no time for anything or anyone. And I knew that I was pretty depressed. I mean I could hardly get up in the morning, and all I could think about was how unhappy I was.

"Like a lot of type A people, I was very aggressive with everyone and not well liked. I don't think I had a single friend at work or anywhere else. I was pushy and loud and obnoxious, and it was making me crazy. I didn't want to be like that, but there I was—unhappy at work, depressed, and about to be single again at 62.

"Things were looking pretty grim at work, and many good people were getting laid off. It didn't feel like it would be very long before the same

thing happened to me, and when my doctor told me my heart was beginning to show serious signs of difficulty, I went for counseling.

"It was hard to do because it meant I had to trust somebody and give
him control of my life. I hated it at first and fought like crazy, but something the therapist said really hit me. He said that the only person I was
hurting by being so disagreeable and argumentative was me, and he was
right. I started to listen and work hard. This was maybe two months into
counseling, and once I did, I felt like I was on the right track. The therapist
used a kind of no-nonsense therapy called cognitive therapy, where you
try and think issues through in a really logical way. It appealed to me. He
was nice enough and all, but he worked my butt off, and he wouldn't let
me get away with any manipulation or angry outbursts.

"I made up with my wife and we started couples counseling with a different therapist. It worked. I found out I really did love my wife. I cut down
on work and started doing fun things I used to think were boring like traveling and hiking and stuff like that. I was such an arrogant bastard that I
used to make fun of people who did those things. My doctor saw me about
three months after I started seeing the therapist. My blood pressure was
much better, and my cholesterol was down too since he wanted me to lose
weight and the therapist helped with that.

"I'm much less depressed than I used to be. It turns out that I was trying to prove myself to my old man, who died 20 years ago. I know that
sounds strange, but a lot of the crazy ideas I had came directly from him,
and a more unhappy and destructive guy I can't imagine. We spent a lot
of time getting his voice out of my head and developing my own thoughts
and ideas about work and life. It wasn't easy. Hell, it was the most difficult
thing I ever did, but it helped a lot.

"I see the therapist once in a while, and I go to a support group for
depressed men. At first I thought the guys in the group were a bunch of
whiners, but as I got to know them better, I realized what great men they
were and how hard they worked to keep themselves from losing it. I con-
fess that I almost lost it and bought a gun, but I threw it away, and now
I try and think of the progress I've made whenever I think life would be
better if I weren't around." —JF

SUMMARY

This chapter on anxiety and depression discussed two important topics
related to the outcomes of work addiction in later life. Help in the form of
counseling and, when needed, medication is quite effective. Two stories
from former clients were provided to help the reader better understand
how counseling works for older work-addicted people facing problems
with anxiety and depression.

REFERENCES

Anxiety

Beck, J.G., & Stanley, M.A. (1997). Anxiety disorders in the elderly: The emerging role of behavior therapy. *Behavior Therapy, 28*, 83–100.

Beekman, A.T., Bremmer, M.A., Deeg, D.J.H., et al. (1998). Anxiety disorders in later life: A report from the Longitudinal Aging Study Amsterdam. *International Journal of Geriatric Psychiatry, 12*, 717–726.

Gallagher-Thompson, D., Hanley-Peterson, P., & Thompson, L.W. (1990). Maintenance of gains versus relapse following brief psychotherapy for depression. *Journal of Consulting and Clinical Psychology, 58*, 371–374.

Kogan, J.N., Edelstein, B.A., & McKee, D.R. (2000). Assessment of anxiety in older adults: Current status. *Journal of Anxiety Disorders, 14*, 109–132.

Lang, A.J., & Stein, M.B. (2001). Anxiety disorders. *Geriatrics, 56*(5), 24–30.

Lawton, M.P. (1977). The impact of the environment on aging and behavior. In. J.E. Birren & K.W. Schaie (Eds.), *Handbook of the psychology of aging* (pp. 276–301). New York: Van Nostrand Reinhold.

Lawton, M.P., & Nahemow, L. (1973). Ecology and the aging process. In C. Eisdorfer & M.P. Lawton (Eds.), *The psychology of adult development and aging* (pp. 619–674). Washington, DC: American Psychological Association.

Pingitore, D., & Sansone, R.A. (1998). Using DSM-IV primary care version: A guide to psychiatric diagnosis in primary care. *American Family Physician, 58*, 23–34.

Robert, S.A., & Li, L.W. (2001). Age variation in the relationship between community socioeconomic status and adult health. *Research on Aging, 23*, 233–258.

Smith, S.S., Sherrill, K.A., & Celenda, C.C. (1995). Anxious elders deserve careful diagnosing and the most appropriate interventions. *Brown University Long-Term Care Letter, 7*(10), 5–7.

Stanley, M.A., & Novy, D.M. (2000). Cognitive-behavior therapy for generalized anxiety in late life: An evaluative overview. *Journal of Anxiety Disorders, 14*, 191–207.

Depression

Blazer, D.G., Hughes, D.C., & George, L.K. (1987). The epidemiology of depression in an elderly community population. *Journal of the American Geriatric Society, 27*, 281–287.

Casey, D.A. (1994). Depression in the elderly. *Southern Medical Journal, 87*, 559–564.

Gallagher-Thompson, D., Hanley-Peterson, P., & Thompson, L.W. (1990). Maintenance of gains versus relapse following brief psychotherapy for depression. *Journal of Consulting and Clinical Psychology, 58*, 371–374.

Hepner, K.A., Rowe, M., Rost, K., Hickey, S.C., Sherbourne, C.D., Ford, D.E., et al. (2007). The effect of adherence to practice guidelines on depression outcomes. *Annals of Internal Medicine, 147*, 320–329.

Kramer, P.D. (2005, April 17). There's nothing deep about depression. *New York Times Magazine,* 50–53.

Lawton, M.P. (1977). The impact of the environment on aging and behavior. In. J.E. Birren & K.W. Schaie (Eds.), *Handbook of the psychology of aging* (pp. 276–301). New York: Van Nostrand Reinhold.

Lawton, M.P., & Nahemow, L. (1973). Ecology and the aging process. In C. Eisdorfer & M.P. Lawton (Eds.), *The psychology of adult development and aging* (pp. 619–674). Washington, DC: American Psychological Association.

Lebowitz, B.D., Pearson, J.D., Schneider, L.S., Reynolds, C.F., III, Alexopoulos, G.S., Bruce, M.L., et al. (1997). Diagnosis and treatment of depression in late life: Consensus statement update. *Journal of the American Medical Association, 278*, 1186–1190.

Mavandadi, I., Sorkin, D.H., Rook, K.S., & Newsom, J.T. (2007). Pain, positive and negative social exchanges, and depressive symptomatology in later life. *Journal of Aging and Health, 19*, 813–830.

Mills, T.L., & Henretta, J.C. (2001). Racial, ethnic, and socio-demographic differences in the level of psychosocial distress among older Americans. *Research on Aging, 23*, 131–152.

Myers, J.E., & Harper, M.C. (2004). Evidence-based effective practices with older adults. *Journal of Counseling and Development, 82*, 207–218.

National Center for Injury Prevention and Control. (2005). *Web-Based Injury Statistics Query and Reporting System (WISQARS)*. Retrieved January 31, 2007, from the Centers for Disease Control and Prevention Web site: http://www.cdc.gov/ncipc/wisqars.

Robert, S.A., & Li, L.W. (2001). Age variation in the relationship between community socioeconomic status and adult health. *Research on Aging, 23*, 233–258. (p. 9)

Roth, A.D., & Fonagy, E. (1996). *What works with whom? A critical review of psychotherapy research.* New York: Guilford Press.

Tyler, K.A., & Hoyt, D.R. (2000). The effects of an acute stressor on depressive symptoms among older adults. *Research on Aging, 22*, 143–164.

Unützer, J., Katon, W., Callahan, C.M., Williams, J.W., Hunkeler, E., Harpole, L., et al. (2001). Successful aging. *American Journal of Psychiatry, 158*, 839–847.

Vaillant, G.E., & Mukamal, K. (2001). Successful aging. *American Journal of Psychiatry, 158*, 839–847.

Wallis, M.A. (2000). Looking at depression through bifocal lenses. *Nursing, 30*, 58–62.

Zalaquett, C.P., & Stens, A.N. (2006). Psychosocial treatments for major depression and dysthymia in older adults: A review of the research literature. *Journal of Counseling and Development, 84*, 192–201.

CHAPTER 11

Substance Abuse

One of the persistent problems facing workaholics as they age is substance abuse. This isn't surprising given the need to deal with work-related stress and the fact that certain medications, particularly anxiety medications, opiates, and pain medications, help reduce feelings of loneliness, social anxiety, and isolation. A major reason for using pain medications is depression. One of the most common symptoms of depression is nonspecific pain. Ironically, alcohol, the most common substance used by workaholics, tends to increase feelings of loneliness and depression, but it is often used by workaholics because it is readily available and tends to provide short-term relief from stress.

Sorocco and Ferrell (2006) suggest two widely held myths regarding alcohol use among older adults: (1) that it is an infrequent problem and (2) that when older adults have drinking problems, treatment success is limited. In fact, according to the authors, "alcohol abuse among older adults is one of the fastest growing health problems facing this country and even a one-time brief encounter of 15 min or less can reduce nondependent problem drinking by more than 20%" (p. 454).

Among those aged 60 to 64 years responding to the national survey on drug use and health sponsored by the Substance Abuse and Mental Health Services Administration (2004), 50 percent used alcohol in the past month, and 35 percent of individuals aged 65 or older used alcohol in the past month; 6.9 percent of adults aged 65 or older reported binge drinking, and 1.8 percent reported heavy drinking. *Binge drinking* is defined as five or more drinks on the same occasion on at least 1 day in the past month, and heavy drinking is defined as five or more drinks on the same occasion on each of 5 or more days in the past 30 days.

Adams, Barry, and Fleming (1996) report that 2 to 15 percent of older adults exhibit symptoms consistent with alcoholism. The estimated use of alcohol increases significantly for primary care patients, where 10 to 15 percent of the older adult patients meet the criteria for problem drinking. Oslin (2004) considers drinking problematic if it leads to physical, social, or emotional problems. Sorocco and Ferrell (2006) estimate that "a minimum of 1 in every 10 older patients in a medical setting most likely suffers from an alcohol problem" (p. 454).

Although the data on older adult alcohol abuse suggest a growing problem, Sorocco and Ferrell (2006) note how difficult it is to pinpoint alcohol abuse in this population. Even though one-third of all heavy drinkers begin their patterns of alcohol abuse after age 60 (Barrick & Connors, 2002), many symptoms of problem drinking mimic physical problems common to this age group, including depression and dementia. Because of stereotypes of older adults by health care professionals, doctors are often unlikely to screen for alcohol problems, particularly in women and patients who are well educated or affluent (which often includes successful workaholics). Because alcohol abuse is still considered a morally offensive problem, clients and their families may feel ashamed to discuss the problem with their physicians. Because of stereotypes that older adults want to be left alone or have few opportunities for happiness, some doctors believe that drinking is one of the few pleasures left to older men and women.

There are a number of health consequences of older adult problem drinking. Oslin (2004) reports that even small to moderate amounts of alcohol can increase the risk of high blood pressure, sleep problems, and malnutrition. The risk of falls increases with alcohol consumption and significantly increases when 14 or more drinks are consumed per week (Mukamal et al., 2004). Older adults are quite vulnerable to the negative effects of alcohol because they take more medications than younger people and are therefore at risk for drug or alcohol interactions. Because of slower metabolic and clearance mechanisms, older people are also more likely to experience adverse drug and alcohol interactions. Onder, et al. (2002) studied alcohol consumption among a population of older adults 65 to 80 years of age and found that even moderate consumption of alcohol increased the risk of a bad drug reaction by 24 percent.

HOW TO TELL IF YOU HAVE A SUBSTANCE ABUSE PROBLEM

Sorocco and Ferrell (2006) report that certain symptoms may suggest the following alcohol problems in older adults: (1) treatment that is not working for a normally treatable medical illness (e.g., hypertension), (2) insomnia or chronic fatigue related to poor sleep, (3) weight loss or malnutrition, and (4) short-term memory problems.

The *Diagnostic and Statistical Manual of Mental Disorders* (DSM-IV; American Psychiatric Association [APA], 1994) uses the following guidelines to determine whether substance use is abusive: (1) frequent use of substances that interfere with functioning and the fulfillment of responsibilities at home, work, school, and elsewhere; (2) use of substances that impair judgment in dangerous situations such as erratic or fast driving; (3) use of substances that may lead to arrest for unlawful behaviors; and (4) substance use that seriously interferes with relations, marriage, child rearing, and other interpersonal responsibilities (APA, 1994). Substance abuse may also lead to slurred speech, lack of coordination, unsteady gait, memory loss, fatigue and depression, feelings of euphoria, and lack of social inhibitions (APA, 1994).

Short Tests   K. E. Miller (2001) reports that two simple questions asked to substance abusers have an 80 percent chance of diagnosing substance abuse: "In the past year, have you ever drank or used drugs more than you meant to?" and "Have you felt you wanted or needed to cut down on your drinking or drug abuse in the past year?" Miller reports that this simple approach has been found to be an effective diagnostic tool in three controlled studies using random samples and laboratory tests for alcohol and drugs in the bloodstream following interviews.

Stewart and Richards (2000) and Bisson, Nadeau, and Demers (1999) suggest that four questions from the Cut, Annoyed, Guilty, and Eye-Opener (CAGE) questionnaire are predictive of alcohol abuse:

1) Cut: Have you ever felt you should cut down on your drinking? 2) Annoyed: Have people annoyed you by criticizing your drinking? 3) Guilty: Have you ever felt guilty about your drinking? 4) Eye-Opener: Have you ever had a drink first thing in the morning (Eye-opener) to steady your nerves or get rid of a hangover? (Bisson et al., 1999, p. 717)

Stewart and Richards (2000) write, "A patient who answers yes to two or more of these questions probably abuses alcohol; a patient who answers yes to one question should be screened further" (p. 56). Unfortunately, many health care workers fail to use tests or interviews to detect substance abuse, and Backer and Walton-Moss (2001) found that fully 20 to 25 percent of all patients with alcohol-related problems were treated medically for the symptoms of alcoholism rather than for the condition itself, and that a diagnosis of alcohol abuse was never made in almost one-fourth of all alcoholics seen for medical treatment.

Pennington, Butler, and Eagger (2000) report that four out of five older patients referred to a psychiatric service with a diagnosis of alcohol abuse were only treated for depression or associated medical problems and not for substance abuse. The authors believe that the reason elderly patients are not adequately screened for alcohol abuse is that "some health professionals harbor a misguided belief that older people should not be advised to give up established habits, or they may be embarrassed to ask older patients personal questions about alcohol use" (p. 183).

Writing about female alcohol abuse, Backer and Walton-Moss (2001) report that "the development and progression of alcoholism is different in women than in men. Women with alcohol problems have higher rates of dual diagnoses, childhood sexual abuse, panic and phobia disorders, eating disorders, posttraumatic stress disorder, and victimization" (p. 13). The authors provide the following differences between male and female alcoholics: because women metabolize alcohol differently than men, women tend to show signs of becoming intoxicated at a later age than men (26.5 vs. 22.7), experience their fist signs of a recognition of alcohol abuse later (27.5 vs. 25), and see loss of control over their drinking later in life (29.8 vs. 27.2). The mortality rate for female alcoholics is 50 to 100 percent higher than it is for men. Liver damage occurs in women in a shorter period of time and with lower amounts of intake of alcohol. Backer and Walton-Moss (2001) report that "female alcoholics have a higher mortality rate from alcoholism than men from suicide, alcohol-related accidents, circulatory disorders, and cirrhosis of the liver" (p. 15). Use of alcohol by women in adolescence is almost equal to that of male adolescents, and while men use alcohol to socialize, women use it to cope with negative moods and are likely to use alcohol in response to specific stressors in their lives (Backer & Walton-Moss, 2001).

Grant and Dawson (1997) report that early use of alcohol is a very strong predictor of lifelong alcoholism and indicate that 40 percent of young adults aged 18–29 years who began drinking before the age of 15 were considered to be alcohol-dependent, as compared to roughly 10 percent who began drinking after the age of 19. Stewart and Richards (2000) conclude that a number of older adult medical problems may have their origins in heavy alcohol and drug use. Head injuries and spinal separations as a result of accidents may have been caused by substance abuse. Because heavy drinkers often fail to eat, they may have nutritional deficiencies that result in psychotic-like symptoms, including abnormal eye movements, confusion, and forgetfulness. Stomach disorders, liver damage, and severe heartburn may have their origins in heavy drinking because alcohol destroys the stomach's mucosal lining. Fifteen percent of all heavy drinkers develop cirrhosis of the liver, and many develop pancreatitis. Weight loss, pneumonia, muscle loss because of malnutrition, and oral cancer have all been associated with heavy drinking. Stewart and Richards (2000) indicate that substance abusers are poor candidates for surgery. Anesthesia and pain medication can delay alcohol withdrawal for up to five days postoperatively.

Stewart and Richards (2000) provide the following blood alcohol levels as measures of the impact of alcohol in screening for abuse:

- 0.05 percent (equivalent to one or two drinks in an average-sized person): impaired judgment, reduced alertness, loss of inhibitions, euphoria

- 0.10 percent: slower reaction times, decreased caution in risk-taking behavior, impaired fine motor control (legal evidence of intoxication in most states starts at 0.10%)
- 0.15 percent: significant and consistent losses in reaction times
- 0.20 percent: function of entire motor area of brain measurably depressed, causing staggering; the individual may be easily angered or emotional
- 0.25 percent: severe sensory and motor impairment
- 0.30 percent: confusion, stupor
- 0.35 percent: surgical anesthesia
- 0.40 percent: respiratory depression; lethal in about half the population
- 0.50 percent: death from respiratory depression (p. 59)

GETTING HELP

In an evaluation of a larger report by *Consumer Reports* on the effectiveness of counseling, Seligman (1995) found that "Alcoholics Anonymous (AA) did especially well, . . . significantly bettering mental health professionals [in the treatment of alcohol and drug-related problems]" (p. 969). Bien, Miller, and Tonigan (1993) found that two or three 10- to 15-minute counseling sessions were often as effective as more extensive interventions with older alcohol abusers. The sessions included motivation-for-change strategies, education, assessment of the severity of the problem, direct feedback, contracting and goal setting, behavioral modification techniques, and the use of written materials such as self-help manuals. Brief interventions have been shown to be effective in reducing alcohol consumption, binge drinking, and the frequency of excessive drinking in problem drinkers, according to Fleming, Barry, Manwell, Johnson, and London (1997).

W. R. Miller and Sanchez (1994) summarize the key components of brief intervention using the abbreviation FRAMES, which stands for "feedback, responsibility, advice, menu of strategies, empathy, and self-efficacy":

1. *Feedback.* Includes an assessment with feedback to the client regarding the client's risk for alcohol problems, her reasons for drinking, the role of alcohol in the patient's life, and the consequences of drinking

2. *Responsibility.* Includes strategies to help clients understand the need to remain healthy, independent, and financially secure; particularly important when working with older clients and clients with health problems and disabilities

3. *Advice.* Includes direct feedback and suggestions to clients to help them cope with their drinking problems and with other life situations that may contribute to alcohol abuse

4. *Menu of strategies.* Includes a list of strategies to reduce drinking and help cope with such high-risk situations as loneliness, boredom, family problems, and lack of social opportunities

5. *Empathy.* Bien et al. (1993) strongly emphasize the need for a warm, empathic, and understanding style of treatment; Miller and Rollnick (1991) found that an empathetic counseling style produced a 77 percent reduction in client drinking, as compared to a 55 percent reduction when a confrontational approach was used

6. *Self-efficacy.* Includes strategies to help clients rely on their inner resources to make changes in their drinking behavior; inner resources may include positive points of view about themselves, helping others, staying busy, and good problem-solving and coping skills

Fleming and Manwell (1998) report that people with alcohol-related problems often receive counseling from primary care physicians or nursing staff in five or fewer standard office visits. The counseling consists of information about the negative impact of alcohol use as well as practical advice regarding ways of reducing alcohol dependence and the availability of community resources. Gentilello, Donovan, Dunn, and Rivara (1995) report that 25 to 40 percent of the trauma patients seen in emergency rooms may be alcohol-dependent. The authors found that a single motivational interview, at or near the time of discharge, reduced drinking levels and readmission for trauma during six months of follow-up.

RECOVERY WITHOUT PROFESSIONAL HELP

The following material on recovery without professional help was first published in Glicken (2005). I thank Sage Publications for permission to reprint this material. (Excerpted from Glicken, M. D. *Improving the effectiveness of the helping professions: An evidence-based approach to practice.* Thousand Oaks, CA: SAGE Publications, 2005. Pp. 174–175. Reprinted with permission.)

Granfield and Cloud (1996) estimate that as many as 90 percent of all problem drinkers never enter treatment and that many end their abuse of alcohol without any form of treatment (Hingson, Scotch, Day, & Culbert, 1980; Roizen, Cahalan, Lambert, Wiebel, & Shanks, 1978; Stall & Biernacki, 1989). Sobell, Sobell, Toneatto, and Leo (1993) report that 82 percent of the alcoholics they studied who terminated their addiction did so by using natural recovery methods that excluded the use professional treatment. As an example of the use of natural recovery techniques, Granfield and Cloud (1996) report that most ex-smokers discontinued their tobacco use without treatment (Peele, 1989), while many addicted substance abusers "mature-out" of a variety of addictions, including heavy drinking and narcotics use (Snow, 1973). Biernacki (1986) reports that people who use natural methods to end their drug addictions utilize a range of strategies, including discontinuing their relationships with drug users, avoiding drug-using environments (Stall & Biernacki, 1989), having new goals and interests in their lives (Peele, 1989), and using friends and family to provide a support network (Biernacki, 1986). Trice and Roman (1970) indicate that self-help groups with substance-abusing clients are particularly helpful because they develop and continue a support network that assists clients in maintaining abstinence and other changed behaviors.

Granfield and Cloud (1996) studied middle-class alcoholics who used natural recovery alone without professional help or the use of self-help groups. Many of the participants in their study felt that some self-help groups were overly religious, while others believed in alcoholism as a disease that suggested a lifetime struggle. The subjects in the study believed that some self-help groups encouraged dependence on the group and that associating with other alcoholics would probably complicate recovery. In summarizing their findings, Granfield and Cloud (1996) report that

> Many [research subjects] expressed strong opposition to the suggestion that they were powerless over their addictions. Such an ideology, they explained, not only was counterproductive but was also extremely demeaning. These respondents saw themselves as efficacious people who often prided themselves on their past accomplishments. They viewed themselves as being individualists and strong-willed. One respondent, for instance, explained that "such programs encourage powerlessness" and that she would rather "trust her own instincts than the instincts of others." (p. 51)

Waldorf, Reinarman, and Murphy (1991) found that many addicted people with jobs, strong family ties, and other close emotional supports were able to walk away from their very heavy use of cocaine. Granfield and Cloud (1996) note that many of the respondents in their study had a great deal to lose if they continued their substance abuse and that their sample consisted of people with stable lives, good jobs, supportive families and friends, college educations, and other social supports that gave them motivation to alter their drug-using behaviors.

A WORKAHOLIC REAL ESTATE AGENT BECOMES A LATE-LIFE ALCOHOLIC: CASE EXAMPLE

Beth Peterson is a 62-year-old single woman who lives in a retirement community in Arizona. Beth was a successful real estate agent in Kansas City for many years and decided to sell her home at the height of the real estate boom in 2005 and buy a home in a retirement community. Beth moved to her new home in January and was ecstatic to find 70-degree weather and many outdoor activities she could not do in Kansas City during the winter. However, her first summer in Arizona was a shock, with temperatures hovering in the 100- to 115-degree range for almost six months without stop.

During the hot months, Beth found that many people left for cooler climates and that her fantasy of many close friends to accompany her on adventures evaporated. She was alone, and there were few people with whom she could socialize. The community had a bar with a happy hour where cheap drinks and food were available, and Beth began going every afternoon at four o'clock and began staying increasingly later.

Beth said she had never been much of a drinker, but after going to happy hour almost every day for a year, she found that thinking about having a drink gave her great joy. She couldn't wait until four o'clock to begin drinking. The bar was only a short distance from her home, and she either walked or drove her electric golf cart there. Driving home from the bar in her cart about 1:00 A.M., when most people were asleep, Beth missed a turn, and her cart went down a steep embankment. She and a friend were to go walking at six o'clock the next morning before the summer heat became unbearable. Not finding Beth at home, the friend contacted security, and after a long search, they found Beth unconscious at the bottom of the embankment with the cart lying partially on top of her.

Beth was rushed to the hospital, and thankfully her injuries were limited to a broken arm and a number of cuts and bruises. More serious was the fact that her blood pressure and blood sugars were extremely high. Wondering about the possibility of an alcohol problem, the attending physician checked her alcohol level and, even after many hours without alcohol, found it high. He also found evidence of beginning liver damage and possible heart problems.

When Beth was fully awake, the doctor and a social worker interviewed her about her accident and her alcohol consumption. At first she was very defensive, but after a few minutes of avoiding their questions, she admitted that she drank 10 to 15 drinks, usually martinis, every day at the bar and had even begun having a few drinks before happy hour. A social worker and nurse met with Beth three additional times over the course of a three-day stay in the hospital. They gave her information about the health impact of drinking and did a screening test to determine Beth's level of abusive drinking. They concluded that she was seriously alcoholic because her drinking impaired her judgment and was thought to be responsible for the high blood pressure and high blood sugar readings consistent with adult-onset diabetes.

A social history taken by the social worker revealed that Beth was painfully lonely and that her drinking seemed to be a response to early retirement without a plan for what she would do with herself after a lifetime of hard, successful work. The history also revealed that Beth had come from a family of alcoholics and that she had vowed to keep her drinking limited but now realized that she was romanticizing about alcohol the way many members of her family had. Beth had her driver's license revoked, and her ability to drive her golf cart on the retirement community grounds was curtailed to daylight hours and only if someone was with her. She was told by the retirement community CEO that bylaws of the community required her to go for counseling and that she had to maintain sobriety for six months before she could have full use of her cart privileges. She was also banned from any of the bars in the retirement community.

Beth met with her substance abuse counselor and for the first few sessions was very angry and could only talk about the hoity-toity CEO, asking, who did he think he was? She'd seen lots of men like him, and she would just like to tell him a thing or two. But on the third session, Beth broke down and cried, telling the counselor that she had made a mistake retiring and leaving her support network in Kansas City. Little did she know, she told the counselor, she had an aversion to "old people" and hated it there in the community. She thought she'd meet a man, but most of the men were either "jerks, and the same Casanovas she'd been meeting most of her life" or too old and sick to be any fun. She'd spent her first 18 years taking care of "drunks," and she never wanted to take care of anyone again. Still, she was lonely, and she was finding that loneliness was everything it was cracked up to be.

The first item on the agenda was to focus on resolving the alcohol problem and the issues that seemed to bring about the late-life drinking problem. After some discussion, Beth pointed out that she didn't like the words *alcoholic* or *drunk* because they were words used to describe members of her family. She did agree that she was drinking too much and that the drinking had physical and mental health implications. The counselor requested that Beth do what she had done so often in her lifetime: take control of her problem by assertively looking for more information that she could use in counseling. Beth agreed, and the counselor gave her a list of articles on the Internet she might read for the next session and encouraged Beth do her own reading about late-life drinking problems, loneliness, and early retirement.

From the work of Kuperman et al. (2001), they agreed that Beth had a number of problems that should be dealt with, including feelings of loneliness, lack of work to keep her occupied, little ability to handle leisure time, and alcohol abuse. The counselor also suggested articles about workaholics because it was clear from her past work history that Beth had been spending so much time working that her social contacts were severely limited. The support group she said she had had in Kansas City was a concoction she used whenever she told people she would have been better off had she stayed in Kansas City. The truth was that she had been painfully lonely and had moved to Arizona because she thought it would improve her life.

Beth and her counselor decided that they would combine a very practical approach to counseling called *cognitive-behavioral therapy* and reading articles the counselor thought would be helpful. Beth also thought that an understanding of the impact her alcoholic family had on her current situation would help.

After months of counseling, during which time Beth would often avoid answering questions directly or would go off on tangents, she began to talk about her feelings and admitted that she was still drinking heavily. She also continued to drive, though her license had been suspended. She felt strong when she drank and loved the peaceful feeling that came over her as she got drunk. Like her parents, she romanticized her drinking and could hardly wait to have her first drink of the day. Sometimes she'd drink when she woke up and often drank rather than eating. She was aware that this cycle of drinking to feel better about herself could only lead to serious life problems, but she didn't think she was capable of stopping. A number of women in the community were secret drinkers, she told the counselor, and drinking was one of the few pleasures they have. Life had stopped having meaning and, faced with many years of living alone and doing nothing, she found solace in alcohol. The counselor made her promise to stop driving because it was illegal and unsafe to Beth and others given her continued drinking.

After a number of sessions of counseling, the counselor admitted to Beth that the treatment wasn't helping Beth with her drinking. Although Beth read articles and came prepared to discuss them, it was an intellectual exercise that wasn't helping Beth change her behavior. Beth pleaded with the counselor not to give up on her. She was the only person in Beth's life with whom she could talk. She didn't know what she would do if the counselor gave up on her and openly considered suicide as an option.

The session was electric as Beth spoke of her early life and her codependency and how it had made relationships impossible. She had lied about her drinking and had a pattern of binge drinking from early adolescence but had never done anything about it. She thought of herself as a tough-minded woman who had lapses, only this lapse wasn't going away. She promised to hunker down and get to work, and she did. On her 64th birthday, she passed six months of sobriety and had her cart privileges returned. With the counselor's recommendation, she also got her driver's license back. She has joined a real estate firm selling resales in the retirement community and is busier than ever—and she has found a man her age who she considers her best friend and companion. In the time she has available after work, they take advantage of the many cultural events in the community. During the hottest months of the summer, they go to the mountains.

Beth's counselor said,

> I want to applaud the professionals Beth worked with in the hospital. Even though the treatment was brief, it made a lasting impact on Beth to hear that she was considered an alcoholic, and it did bring her into treatment along with the loss of her license and the recognition in the retirement community that she had a drinking problem. That's exactly what you hope for in serious alcoholics who are in denial. It took Beth longer to turn the corner and get down to work than younger adults. The reason for this delay, I've come to believe, because I see the same thing in other older substance abusers, is a sense of hopelessness in many older adults. They accept cultural stereotypes that older people have no useful function, and they tend to give up. They also think that retirement will be a magical time when they'll meet interesting people, have intimate relationships, and be active much of the

time. That isn't always the case, and many people retire before they are ready because they're burned out and angry about their personal lives. They don't realize that work gives them a schedule and fills in free time that many older adults haven't learned to handle.

I'm never surprised when people tell me that they have a history of drinking even though they deny it early in treatment. I wonder about late-onset alcoholism, and though I'm sure it exists, many older people with no actual history of drinking problems find alcohol aversive both in taste and in its effect. I think Beth is one of many tough-minded, successful women in our society who fill their lives so full that when they take a break and try to relax, many emotional issues come up they'd rather not deal with. So they work extra hard, have lots of acquaintances, and stay very busy. When they retire, many years of denial and ignoring problems begin to have an impact. The fact that Beth read the articles I suggested and came prepared to discuss them gave her a large body of information. When she was ready to begin changing, the material she'd read came in very handy.

I don't want to define Beth as a success story. Alcohol isn't her only problem. When she becomes too tired to work or fill up her time with other activities, it wouldn't surprise me if she had a relapse. Right now, she's had a scare and she's very motivated. I've referred her for more in-depth counseling that will help her understand the impact of her early life, but she's put it off. I suspect she's had some very bad traumas, and maybe she can avoid discussing them, but I think sooner or later, they'll come back to haunt her.

SUMMARY

Substance abuse is a very real problem for older work-addicted people. The chapter discussed the reasons for using substances, tests one can use to determine if someone has a substance abuse problem, effective treatments, and a case study of a work-addicted woman who retired and developed a serious late-life drinking problem. Alcohol in particular has a very negative impact on health, particularly in women and older adults, and early physical signs of alcohol abuse include high blood pressure and late life-onset diabetes. Both are serious problems with major health ramifications. Workaholics are particularly at risk for substance abuse and the many health consequences associated with alcohol and drug abuse.

REFERENCES

Adams, W.L., Barry, K.L., & Fleming, M.F. (1996). Screening for problem drinking in older primary care patients. *Journal of the American Medical Association, 276*, 1964–1967.

American Psychiatric Association. (1994). *Diagnostic and statistical manual of mental disorders* (4th ed.). Washington, DC: Author.

Backer, K.L., & Walton-Moss, B. (2001). Detecting and addressing alcohol abuse in women. *Nurse Practitioner, 26*(10), 13–22.

Barrick, C., & Connors, G.J. (2002). Relapse prevention and maintaining abstinence in older adults with alcohol-use disorders. *Drugs and Aging, 19*, 583–594.

Bien, T.J., Miller, W.R., & Tonigan, J.S. (1993). Brief interventions for alcohol problems: A review. *Addictions, 88*, 315–335.

Biernacki, P. (1986). *Pathways from heroin addiction: Recover without treatment*. Philadelphia: Temple University Press.

Bisson, J., Nadeau, L., & Demers, A. (1999). The validity of the CAGE scale to screen heavy drinking and drinking problems in a general population. *Addiction, 94*, 715–723.

Fleming, M.F., Barry, K.L., Manwell, L.B., Johnson, K., & London, R. (1997). Brief physician advice for problem alcohol drinkers: A randomized controlled trial in community-based primary care practices. *Journal of the American Medical Association, 277*, 1039–1045.

Fleming, M., & Manwell, L.B. (1998). Brief intervention in primary care settings: A primary treatment method for at-risk, problem, and dependent drinkers. *Alcohol Research and Health, 23*, 128–137.

Gentilello, L.M., Donovan, D.M., Dunn, C.W., & Rivara, F.P. (1995). Alcohol interventions in trauma centers: Current practice and future directions. *Journal of the American Medical Association, 274*, 1043–1048.

Glicken, M.D. (2005). *Improving the effectiveness of the helping professions: An evidence-based approach to practice*. Thousand Oaks, CA: Sage.

Granfield, R., & Cloud, W. (1996). The elephant that no one sees: Natural recovery among middle-class addicts. *Journal of Drug Issues, 26*, 45–61.

Grant, B.F., & Dawson, D.A. (1997). Age at onset of alcohol use and its association with DSM-IV alcohol abuse and dependence: Results from the National Longitudinal Alcohol Epidemiologic Survey. *Journal of Substance Abuse, 9*, 103–110.

Hingson, R., Scotch, N., Day, N., & Culbert, A. (1980). Recognizing and seeking help for drinking problems. *Journal of Studies on Alcohol, 41*, 1102–1117.

Kuperman, S., Schlosser, S.S., Kramer, J.R., Bucholz, K., Hesselbrock, V., Reich, T., & Reich, W. (2001, April). Risk domains associated with adolescent alcohol dependence diagnosis. *Addiction, 96*(4), 629–637.

Miller, K.E. (2001). Can two questions screen for alcohol and substance abuse? *American Family Physician, 64*, 1247–1286.

Miller, W.R., & Roilnick, S. (1991). *Motivational interviewing: preparing people for change*. New York: Guilford Press.

Miller, W.R., & Sanchez, V.C. (1994). Motivating young adults for treatment and lifestyle change. In G.S. Howard & P.E. Nathan (Eds.), *Alcohol use and misuse by young adults* (pp. 55–81). Notre Dame, IN: University of Notre Dame Press.

Mukamal, K.J., Mittleman, M.A., Longstreth, W.T., Newman, A.B., Eried, L.P., & Siscovick, D.S. (2004). Self-reports alcohol consumption and falls in older adults: Cross-sectional and longitudinal analyses of the cardiovascular health study. *Journal of the American Geriatrics Society, 52*, 1174–1179. (In Text)

Onder, G., Landi, E., Delia Vedova, C., Atkinson, H., Pedone, C., Cesari, M., et al. (2002). Moderate alcohol consumption and adverse drug reactions among older adults. *Pharmacoepidemiological Drug Safety, 11*, 385–392.

Oslin, D.W. (2004). Late-life alcoholism: Issues relevant to the geriatric psychiatrist. *American Journal of Geriatric Psychiatry, 12*, 571–583.

Peele, S. (1989). *The diseasing of America: Addiction treatment out of control.* Lexington, MA: Lexington Books.

Pennington, H., Butler, R., & Eagger, S. (2000). The assessment of patients with alcohol disorders by an old age psychiatric service. *Aging and Mental Health, 4*, 182–185.

Roizen, R., Cahalan, D., Lambert, E., Wiebel, W., & Shanks, P. (1978). Spontaneous remission among untreated problem drinkers. In D. Kandel (Ed.), *Longitudinal research on drug use* (pp. 143–196). Washington, DC: Hemisphere.

Seligman, M.E.P. (1995). The effectiveness of psychotherapy: The *Consumer Reports* study. *American Psychologist, 50*, 965–974.

Snow, M. (1973). Maturing out of narcotic addiction in New York City. *International Journal of the Addictions, 8*, 932–938.

Sobell, L., Sobell, M., Toneatto, T., & Leo, G. (1993). What triggers the resolution of alcohol problems without treatment? *Alcoholism: Clinical and Experimental Research, 17*, 217–224.

Sorocco, K.H., & Ferrell, S.W. (2006). Alcohol use among older adults. *The Journal of General Psychology, 133*(4), 453–467.

Stall, R., & Biernacki, P. (1989). Spontaneous remission from the problematic use of substances. *International Journal of the Addictions, 21*, 1–23.

Stewart, K.B., & Richards, A.B. (2000). Recognizing and managing your patient's alcohol abuse. *Nursing, 30*, 56–60.

Substance Abuse and Mental Health Services Administration. (2004). *2004 national survey on drug use and health.* Rockville, MD: U.S. Department of Health and Human Services.

Trice, H., & Roman, P. (1970). Delabeling, relabeling, and Alcoholics Anonymous. *Social Problems, 17*, 538–546.

Waldorf, D., Reinarman, C., & Murphy, S. (1991). *Cocaine changes: The experience of using and quitting.* Philadelphia: Temple University Press.

CHAPTER 12

Health

Work-addicted people have reason to be concerned about their health as they age because of work-related stress, the inability to use weekends and vacations as times to wind down and relax, and the general belief that workaholics, particularly men, will have serious health problems that are especially likely to occur as they age. Just looking at the following problems of men, whether they are work addicted or not, you can see the problems that work-addicted men will have as they age.

In reporting data from the University of Michigan's Institute for Social Research, Gupta (2003) notes that "men outrank women in all of the 15 leading causes of death, except one: Alzheimer's. Men's death rates are at least twice as high as women's for suicide, homicide and cirrhosis of the liver" (p. 84). The principal researcher on the study of men's health, David Williams, says that men are twice as likely to be heavy drinkers and to "engage in behaviors that put their health at risk, from abusing drugs to driving without a seat belt" (Gupta, 2003, p. 84). Gupta goes on to note that men are more often involved in risky driving and that SUV rollovers and motorcycle accidents largely involve men. Williams (as cited in Gupta, 2003) blames this behavior on "deep-seated cultural beliefs—a 'macho' world view that rewards men for taking risks and tackling danger head on" (p. 84).

Further examples of risky male behavior leading to injury and death are that men are twice as likely to get hit by lightning; die in a flash flood; drive around barricades, resulting in more deaths by train accidents; and drown in high water. Gupta also reports that women are twice as likely as men to visit their doctor once a year and are more likely to explore broad-based preventive health plans with their physicians than men. Men are less likely to schedule checkups or to follow up when symptoms arise. Men also tend to bottle up their emotions and self-medicate their emotional problems, notes Williams, while women tend to seek professional help. Virtually all stress-related diseases—from hypertension to heart disease—are more common in men.

Saunders (2000) reports that a poll by Louis Harris and Associates in May and November 1998 indicated that 28 percent of the men, as compared to 8 percent of the women, had not visited a physician in the prior year. While 19 percent of the women didn't have a regular physician, 33 percent of men didn't have one either. More than half of the men surveyed had not had a screening test for cholesterol or a physical examination in the prior year. Waiting as long as possible to receive needed medical care was a strategy used by one-fourth of the men surveyed. Only 18 percent of the men surveyed sought medical care immediately when a medical problem arose.

Additional health data paint an equally troubling picture of men's health. *Drug Store News* (1998) reports the following information for American pharmacists: (1) women still outlive men by an average of six to seven years, despite advances in medical technology; (2) the death rate from prostate cancer has increased by 23 percent since 1973; (3) oral cancer related to smoking occurs more than twice as often in men; (4) three times as many men suffer heart attacks than women before age 65 (nearly three in four coronary artery bypasses in 1995 were performed on men); (5) bladder cancer occurs five times more often in men than in women; (6) nearly 95 percent of all DWI cases involve men; and (7) in 1970, the suicide rate for white men was 9.4 per 100,000, as compared to 2.9 per 100,000 for white women. By 1986, the rate for white males had risen to 18.2 per 100,000, as compared to 4.1 per 100,000 for women, and by 1991, the rate for white male suicide was 19.3 per 100,000, as compared to a slight increase to 4.3 per 100,000 for women. In 1991, suicide rates for black and Latino men were 11.5 per 100,000 or almost six times the rate of suicide for black and Latino women, whose rate was 2 per 100,000.

WHY MEN HAVE MORE HEALTH PROBLEMS THAN WOMEN

Harrison, Chin, and Ficarrotto (1988) believe that as much as three-fourths of the seven-year difference in life expectancy between men and women is attributable to socialization. Though parents often believe that boys are tougher than girls, in reality, they are far more vulnerable to illness and disease than female children. Male children are more likely to develop a variety of behavioral difficulties such as hyperactivity, stuttering, dyslexia, and learning disorders. There seems to be little evidence that these behavioral health problems experienced by boys are genetically determined. In explaining the difference in health data between men and women, Harrison et al. write that "male socialization into aggressive behavioral patterns seems clearly related to the higher death rate from external causes. Male anxiety about the achievement of masculine status seems to result in a variety of behaviors that can be understood as compensatory" (p. 276), a concept Harrison et al. explain as follows:

One way children cope with anxiety derived from sex-role expectations is the development of compensatory masculinity. Compensatory masculinity behaviors range from the innocent to the insidious. Boys naturally imitate the male models available to them and can be observed overemphasizing male gait and male verbal patterns. But if the motive is the need to prove the right to male status, more destructive behavioral patterns may result, and persist into adulthood. Boys are often compelled to take risks that result in accidents; older youth often begin smoking and drinking as a symbol of adult male status; automobiles are often utilized as an extension of male power; and some men find confirmation of themselves in violence toward those whom they do not consider confirming their male roles. (p. 298)

In reporting the health consequences of compensatory masculinity, Karlberg, Unden, Elofsson, and Krakau (1998) studied type A behavior and its relationship to automobile accidents. Type A behavior has been studied extensively for its impact on coronary heart disease and includes several components that the authors found to be risk factors for automobile accidents: impatience; easily aroused irritability; hostility; and always being in a hurry, even when hurrying is unnecessary. The authors found that men with type A behavior had higher rates of automobile accidents when in a hurry than women with similar personality traits. Aaron et al. (1985) found a strong relationship between type A behavior and alcohol ingestion in a study of 12,886 men aged 35 to 57 years. The authors concluded that type A men have a high need for relaxation that makes them more inclined to drink alcohol and use drugs.

In noting the many differences in health-related behaviors between men and women, Courtenay (2000) reports that "men's behavior is a major—if not the primary—determinant of their excess mortality and premature deaths. Furthermore, this review reveals that the leading causes of disease and death among men are clearly linked to over 30 behaviors and lifestyle habits that are controllable and can be modified" (p. 100).

Among those negative behaviors, the author notes the following: combining alcohol with drugs and smoking, which increases the risk of cancer by 15 times; unbelted driving, which increases the risk of brain injury and other disabilities; violent behavior and fighting; lack of regular health checkups; a continuation of unhealthy lifestyles, including obesity, lack of exercise, and the tendency to self-medicate; lack of the use of vitamins; less sleep or less quality sleep than women, which increases the risk of

accidents and health problems; lack of helmet use when driving motorcy-
cles; risky sexual behavior leading to STDs, including AIDS; an unwilling-
ness to use sun protection to prevent skin cancer; the underuse of dietary
fiber and the overuse of fat, which often leads to cardiovascular problems
in men; the use of anabolic steroids in sports and weight training, which
increases the risk of cardiovascular disease and cancer; dangerous jobs that
require unsafe risk taking (though males constitute only a little over half
of the workforce, they account for 94% of fatal injuries on the job; National
Institute for Occupational Safety and Health, 1993); unsafe driving, driving
while under the influence of alcohol or drugs, and driving without proper
use of safety equipment; involvement in risky sports and recreation; crimi-
nal activity (men are involved in 85% of the crimes in America); and unemployment, underemployment, and job discrimination.

To help reduce the risk of poor health and early death among men,
Courtenay (1996) suggests the use of a health-risk assessment that includes
physical and emotional indicators of at-risk behavior and that medical and
psychological personnel use this type of assessment to help men deal with
risky behaviors that needlessly affect their health and are avoidable. Among
the assessment items would be information pertaining to the following:
(1) satisfaction with work, personal life, and relationships; (2) work-related
problems, including work addiction, frequent job changes, fighting, or
sexual harassment charges; (3) the date of the last health checkup and if
any problems were noted; (4) how often a physician was seen and under
what circumstances; (5) weight, amount of exercise, and caloric/fat intake;
(6) existence of serious health problems in a man's biological family; (7) involvement in risky sports or recreation; (8) number of times married or
divorced; (9) financial problems; (10) average amount of alcohol or illicit
drugs consumed per week; (11) all current prescription and over-the-
counter drugs taken; (12) indications of metabolic syndrome (high blood
sugars, high blood pressure readings, waist size greater than 36, and high
cholesterol, all of which are related to cardiovascular problems in men);
(13) sexual history including STDs, unprotected sex, number of sexual
partners, recent sexual activity, erectile problems, or other sexual problems; (14) last prostate checkup; (15) smoking history; (16) level of danger at work or the existence of dangerous chemicals in the workplace; and
(17) length of work commute.

Additional assessment items include the following: (1) average number
of hours of sleep per night; (2) history of violent behavior, including fights
and domestic violence; (3) evidence of problems with temper and/or irritability; (4) problems with depression or anxiety; (5) prior experience with
therapy, if any, and for what reasons; (6) early-life health or emotional
problems, including fighting, abuse, gang membership, fire setting, and
other problems that might suggest early-life trauma; (7) history of accidents or brain injuries; (8) history of abusing children; (9) prior surgeries
or medical problems; (10) number of close friends and how often they are

seen; (11) life span of parents or their current age, if alive; and (12) educational level and achievement (grades).

Personal Story: A Money Manager Retires because of Health Problems (What Happens When the Fire in the Belly Leaves?)

"Where does that fire in the belly go when your daily routine is abruptly changed?

"After running my money management company for 21 years, I was told that stress was going to kill me. I could no longer use statins [anticholesterol medications] to fight the buildup of plaque in my arteries, and my doctor told me that a wellness plan was my only fight against heart disease. The wellness plan included vitamins, enzymes, lots of exercise, and a change of lifestyle.

"Could I do that? My workday revolved around the hours of Wall Street and also two hours before trading began and the early-morning hours of Asian trading. My mind was always on. I tracked currencies, commodities, bonds, and equities. I lived and breathed the markets. The early-morning hours where I lived on the West Coast were my prime working hours. Biologically, those are the hours when cortisol runs rampant in my bloodstream, and to dissipate its negative effect on my arteries, exercise was my only defense. [Author's note regarding cortisol: when it functions normally, cortisol helps maintain energy when it is needed. Sustained high cortisol levels destroy healthy muscle and bone; slow down healing and normal cell regeneration; co-opt biochemicals needed to make other vital hormones; impair digestion, metabolism, and mental function; interfere with healthy endocrine function; and weaken the immune system.]

"I had spent the past 28 years helping others to prepare financially for retirement, and here I was abruptly jumping into retirement. During those working years, I was totally absorbed in my business and the markets. While not working, I coached my son's sports teams and volunteered in the schools and at various nonprofit organizations. I always had something to channel my energies.

"While helping others plan for retirement, I noticed how so many type A individuals never emotionally approached the issue of retirement. In my mind, I was never really going to retire; downsizing my business had been my plan for the past 15 years. Retaining some clients, perhaps a handful, was my retirement plan. Yet now that I have leaped into retirement, how was I going to fill the emotional side, the gratification of doing a fine job that I received from my efforts?

"The daily excitement of making money for my clients and myself was the fire in my belly that propelled me up the mountain of success. From 1988 to 1999, I never took a vacation where I was not in touch with my office and the movements of the stock market. In 1999, I went to Africa, and for the first time in 11 years, I had a vacation. Being away from it all meant I was free to channel my energies into the world around me. It is easy to be excited when one is on a safari. The meaning of *safari* is to be on a journey. While in Africa, my journey was not only observing animal behavior and meeting new people but also a time of self-discovery. Two additional trips to Africa had the same effect on me. I was totally absorbed by my surroundings.

"On reflection, my challenge will be to get excited, *fired up* about new projects. I have moved to a new community. On this new safari, my hope is that a new environment will enhance my survival skills. Surviving, for me, is more than putting three meals on the table. It is becoming part of the community. Newcomers have to reach out to new neighbors, mingle, join new organizations and clubs, and put energy into new relationships.

"On my life's journey, I have been a caregiver. Will I be able to find a way to care for myself? Every day that I allow to slip away and not be proactive in caring for myself, I ask myself this question: have I come here to live or to die? Sometimes I don't get an answer. Admittedly, I am struggling, but that is part of the journey."—Barry Kravitz, Santa Barbara, California, and Prescott, Arizona

TAKING CARE OF YOURSELF: SOME GENERAL ADVICE

Through their research on successful aging, Vaillant and Mukamal (2001) believe that we can identify the predictors of longer and healthier lives before the age of 50 by using the following indicators: (1) parental social class, (2) family cohesion, (3) lack of major depression, (4) ancestral longevity, (5) childhood temperament, and (6) physical health at age 50. Six variables indicating personal control over physical and emotional health that are also related to longer and healthier lives include the following: (1) absence of alcohol abuse and smoking, (2) the presence of marital/relationship stability, (3) exercise, (4) normal body mass index, (5) positive coping mechanisms, and (6) involvement in continuing education. The authors conclude that we have much greater control over our postretirement health than had been previously recognized in the literature.

A number of researchers writing about older adults discuss the concept of successful aging. In his research on aging, Vaillant (2002) found that the following contributed to successful aging: (1) seeking and maintaining quality relationships; (2) having interest and concern for others and being able to give of oneself; (3) having a sense of humor and the ability to laugh and play well into later life; (4) making new friends as we lose older ones (Valiant found that quality friendships have a more positive impact on aging well than retirement income); (5) maintaining a desire to learn and to be open to new ideas and new points of view; (6) understanding and accepting our limitations and, when necessary, accepting the help of others; (7) understanding the past and its effect on our lives, while living in the present; and (8) focusing on the positives and the good people in our lives rather than on the negative things that may happen to us.

In the next three sections, three serious problems that affect work-addicted people will be discussed, with particular attention paid to prevention: heart problems, diabetes, and Alzheimer's disease. These three problems were chosen because there are ways to prevent them from occurring even in those of you whose stress levels and inability to relax cause you to be more at risk than the population at large.

PREVENTING HEART PROBLEMS

The following information is summarized from the American Heart Association (2008) and Mayo Clinic (2008) Web sites:

1. *Don't smoke or use tobacco products.* When it comes to heart disease prevention, no amount of smoking is safe. Tobacco smoke contains more than 4,800 chemicals. Many of these can damage your heart and blood vessels, making them more vulnerable to narrowing of the arteries (atherosclerosis). Atherosclerosis can ultimately lead to a heart attack.

   In addition, the nicotine in cigarette smoke makes your heart work harder by constricting blood vessels and increasing your heart rate and blood pressure. Carbon monoxide in cigarette smoke replaces some of the oxygen in your blood. This increases your blood pressure by forcing your heart to work harder to supply enough oxygen. The good news, though, is that when you quit smoking, your risk of heart disease drops dramatically within just one year. And no matter how long or how much you smoked, you'll start reaping rewards as soon as you quit.

2. *Get active.* Regularly participating in moderately vigorous physical activity can reduce your risk of fatal heart disease by nearly a quarter. And when you combine physical activity with other lifestyle measures, such as maintaining a healthy weight, the payoff is even greater.

   Regular physical activity helps prevent heart disease by increasing blood flow to your heart and strengthening your heart's contractions so that your heart pumps more blood with less effort. Physical activity also helps you control your weight and can reduce your chances of developing other conditions that may put a strain on your heart such as high blood pressure, high cholesterol, and diabetes. It also reduces stress, which may be a factor in heart disease.

   Federal guidelines recommend that you get at least 30 to 60 minutes of moderately intense physical activity most days of the week. However, even shorter amounts offer heart benefits, so if you can't meet those guidelines, don't give up. And remember that things like gardening, housekeeping, taking the stairs, and walking the dog all count toward your total. You don't have to exercise strenuously to achieve benefits, but you can see bigger benefits by increasing the intensity, duration, and frequency of your workouts.

3. *Eat a heart-healthy diet.* Consistently eating a diet rich in fruits, vegetables, whole grains and low-fat dairy products can help protect your heart. Legumes, low-fat sources of protein, and certain types of fish also can reduce your risk of heart disease. Saturated, polyunsaturated, monounsaturated, and trans fats increase the risk of coronary artery disease by raising blood cholesterol levels. Major sources of saturated fat include beef, butter, cheese, milk, and coconut and palm oils. There's growing evidence that trans fats may be worse than saturated fats because unlike saturated fat, they both raise your LDL (bad) cholesterol and lower your HDL (good) cholesterol. Sources of trans fats include deep-fried fast foods, bakery products, packaged snack foods, margarines, and crackers.

Omega-3 fatty acids may decrease your risk of heart attack, protect against an irregular heartbeat, and lower blood pressure. Some fish are a good natural source of omega-3s. Omega-3s are present in smaller amounts in flaxseed oil, walnut oil, soybean oil, and canola oil, and they can also be found in supplements.

Following a heart-healthy diet also means drinking alcohol only in moderation—no more than two drinks a day for men, one a day for women. At that moderate level, alcohol can have a protective effect on your heart. Above that, it becomes a health hazard.

Researchers in England find promise in broccoli, which has been found to repair heart damage caused by diabetes by producing an enzyme that protects heart vessels. Previous research has shown broccoli linked to a lower risk of heart attack and stroke. Not many of us like broccoli, but this type of evidence suggests that we should add it to our diet not only as a preventative measure but also as a way of developing good heart health if you are diabetic.

4. *Maintain a healthy weight.* As you put on weight in adulthood, you gain mostly fatty tissue. This excess weight can lead to conditions that increase your chances of heart disease such as high blood pressure, high cholesterol, and diabetes.

How do you know if your weight is healthy? In general, men are considered overweight if their waist measurement is greater than 40 inches. And women, in general, are overweight if their waist measurement is greater than 35 inches. Even small reductions in weight can be beneficial. Reducing your weight by just 10 percent can decrease your blood pressure, lower your blood cholesterol level, and reduce your risk of diabetes. Weight loss also lessens pressure on knees, back, ankles, and feet that can prevent considerable discomfort as we age.

5. *Get regular health screenings.* High blood pressure and high cholesterol can damage your cardiovascular system, including your heart. But without testing for them, you probably won't know whether you have these conditions. Regular screening can tell you what your numbers are and whether you need to take action. Adults should have their blood pressure checked often. Inexpensive blood pressure machines are available at many discount stores. If you are work addicted, you need to check your blood pressure at least several times a week.

Adults should have their cholesterol measured at least once every five years. You may need more frequent testing if your numbers aren't optimal or if you have other risk factors for cardiovascular disease. Some children may need their blood cholesterol tested if they have a strong family history of heart disease.

6. *Aspirin and heart health.* A low dose of aspirin (50 milligrams) appears to be just as effective as a higher dose (325 milligrams) in preventing heart attack, stroke, or death among patients with stable cardiovascular disease, according to researchers at Duke University Medical Center (2008). In reviewing data from nearly 10,000 patients enrolled in these trials, researchers discovered that those who took aspirin daily had a 25 percent reduction in the risk of stroke, a 26 percent reduction in the risk of a second heart attack, and a 13 percent lower risk of death when compared with people who took a placebo. Overall, in considering all types of cardiovascular events, patients who took aspirin were 21 percent less likely to encounter potentially fatal problems than those who did not. We also know that aspirin can prevent recurrence of colon cancer.

PREVENTING DIABETES

Although there are many reasons for the high rates of diabetes among older adults, including heredity, pancreatic disease, and cardiovascular problems, the primary reason is obesity coupled with inactivity and a diet high in carbohydrates. Like many of us, a friend began putting on weight in his 50s, although he was still an avid tennis player. He was told by doctors for about five years that his blood sugar readings were too high before he did anything about it. Six months before he was diagnosed with type 2 (non-insulin-dependent) diabetes, he said that he was about 60 pounds overweight and not very active.

His doctor called to say his three-month average blood sugars (called a hemoglobin A1C test) were high. How high? They were at 7.8, or an average blood sugar of 170 to 180 (normal is 100 and below). He said he had promised himself that he would lose weight, but that was easier said than done. Five months later, he got violently ill and discovered that his blood sugars had risen to 260, a seriously high number. He was placed on a well-known diabetes medication called metformin and also promptly lost 40 pounds.

Within two months, his blood sugars were around 100 fasting in the morning. He returned to tennis, began hiking, and started a diet low in carbohydrates (sugar). He'd still like to lose 20 pounds, but "it's tough," he told me, "since weight loss isn't that easy, but I had a real scare and it's had a positive impact on my health." He no longer needs diabetes medication. His waist size has dropped from 44 to 38 inches. He plays two hours of singles tennis against much younger opponents and feels healthier than he has in years. He's stopped drinking alcohol because the thought of it is repugnant to him. Having gone to a diabetes dietician, he follows her advice and feels content with his diet.

Preventing diabetes involves the following:

1. Keeping your weight at its suggested level

2. Being active every day for an hour

3. Following a healthy low-fat, low-carbohydrate diet

4. Not smoking and drinking only small amounts of alcohol

5. Keeping stress in check

6. Having your blood sugars checked periodically (you can buy blood sugar monitors cheaply and check your blood sugars in the morning when you wake up and before dinner; if your readings are often above 120, see your doctor as this is a sign that something's wrong)

Additionally, if your blood pressure is high, your waist is over 40 inches for men or 35 inches for women, and your cholesterol is high, then you're at very high risk for heart difficulties.

PREVENTING ALZHEIMER'S DISEASE

One of the most disturbing illnesses associated with aging is Alzheimer's disease (AD). Although the risk factors for developing this disease increase as we age, there are promising new data suggesting that it may be possible to limit that risk.

The Alzheimer's Association (2009) estimates that as many as 4.5 million Americans suffer from AD. The disease usually begins after age 60, and risk goes up with age. While younger people may also get AD, it is much less common. About 5 percent of men and women aged 65 to 74 have AD, and nearly half of those over the age of 85 may have the disease, with the number of people with the disease doubling every five years beyond age 65. Of the over 4 million Americans estimated to have an intellectual decline because of AD, one-third have severe dementia and are so impaired that they can no longer manage without assistance in the simplest daily activities, including eating, dressing, grooming, and toileting.

The symptoms of dementia include loss of memory, extreme mood changes, and communication problems, which include a decline in the ability to talk, write, and read. Though AD is the most common disease in which dementia is a symptom, people with dementia may suffer from the effects of stroke and heart problems causing brain damage because of oxygen deprivation. Dementia can also result, to a lesser extent, from the conditions of multiple sclerosis, motor neuron disease, Parkinson's disease, and Huntington's disease.

Brain fitness activities, including crossword puzzles and a number of computer games, are thought to decrease the risk of AD. Physical activity and aerobic exercise are also believed to protect cognition and benefit memory in midlife (Colcombe et al., 2006). Carle (2007) discusses several brain-training games such as Nana Technology, Posit Science, Mindfit, and MyBrainTrainer.com, in which he describes programs that are "more than just a game" to maintain cognitive strength among older adults.

Scarmeas, Stern, Tang, Mayeux, and Luchsinger (2006) found that people who eat a Mediterranean diet including fruit, vegetables, olive oil, legumes, cereals, and fish experience a lower probability of developing AD. In their study, none of the 2,000 participants with an average age of 76 had AD at the start of the beginning of the study. After four years, only 260 people were diagnosed with AD. The more closely people followed the Mediterranean diet, the less likely they were to develop AD.

Lunde (2008) found growing evidence that exercise not only helps the heart and reduces weight but also lowers one's chances of developing AD. Lunde found that 30 minutes of exercise that increases heart activity done at least several times a week can lower the risk of developing AD. Regular exercise, according to the author, is the best way to prevent AD—better than drugs, thinking activities such as crossword puzzles, and specialized diets.

A promising but preliminary study suggests that elderly people who view themselves as self-disciplined, organized achievers may have a lower risk for developing AD than people who are less conscientious (Wilson, Schneider, Arnold, Bienias, & Bennett, 2007). According to the researchers, a strong self-directed personality may somehow protect the brain, perhaps by increasing neural connections that can act as a reserve against mental decline. Surprisingly, when the brains of some of the strongly self-directed people in the study were autopsied after their deaths, they were found to have lesions that would meet accepted criteria for AD—even though these people had shown no signs of dementia. The authors point out that prior studies have linked social connections and stimulating activities like working puzzles with a lower risk of AD, while people who experience more distress and worry about their lives are at a higher risk.

At the start of the study, none of the participants (997 older Roman Catholic priests, nuns, and brothers who participated in the Religious Orders Study) showed signs of dementia. The average age was 75. The subjects were given IQ tests and tests to measure self-direction (conscientiousness) and then were tracked for 12 years, with testing done yearly to determine if there were signs of cognitive decline and dementia. Brain autopsies were performed on most of those who died.

Over the 12 years, 176 people developed AD, but those with the highest scores for conscientiousness at the start of the study had an 89 percent lower risk of developing AD compared to people with the lowest scores for that personality trait. The conscientiousness scores were based on how people rated themselves on a scale of 0 to 4 on how much they agreed with statements such as "I work hard to accomplish my goals," "I strive for excellence in everything I do," "I keep my belongings clean and neat," and "I'm pretty good about pacing myself so as to get things done on time."

When the researchers took into account a combination of risk factors, including smoking, inactivity, and limited social connections, they still found that the conscientious people had a 54 percent lower risk of AD compared to people with the lowest scores for conscientiousness. While these results are very promising because they seem to indicate that people with high expectations of themselves suffer far less chance of developing AD, it should be noted that the social and physical environments of the subjects (all members of religious communities) contain protective factors that may inhibit or delay the development of AD. Still, this is an exciting study because it suggests that strong personality traits related to conscientiousness should be encouraged and supported in children at early stages of development.

Researchers at the University of North Dakota (Pedraza, 2008) have been studying the link between diets that are high in fat and the onset of AD. They found that one cup of coffee a day can neutralize the impact of fat on brain functioning, and while the relationship between coffee and AD isn't conclusive, the researchers are optimistic that coffee reduces high levels of iron and cholesterol in the brain that have been associated with AD.

Personal Story: A University Professor Uses Phased Retirement because of Health Reasons

"My situation centered around the nature of my job as a professor of music and the wear and tear that I felt after years of taking choral groups of young people on tour. In my early 60s, my doctor noticed that whenever I had returned from a tour, my blood pressure had elevated. Although I loved my young singers and the music we performed, considering health issues and the suspicion that I was burning out, I spoke to my academic dean and suggested that I retire at age 65.

"At Grinnell College [in Grinnell, Iowa] in the 1980s and early 1990s, it was school policy to ask senior professors to retire at 65 or lose some of the college's perks. At age 70, retirement was mandatory [since then, Congress has said that forced retirement would no longer be legally allowed]. However, a carrot-and-stick rule made the transition palatable wherein one would receive 75 percent of one's full-time salary until age 70, using the time in between for research.

"In retrospect, I most likely would not have continued working to age 70 because of my hypertension problem and feeling burned out. Even though the college had a very good retirement plan, and the 75 percent of full pay for five years was generous, as one of my older colleagues told me, the administration just wanted to get rid of us older faculty. And I did feel that administration just wanted to move the old guys out. To be fair,

Grinnell College, in general, does try to keep in touch with its emeritus professors.

"I did find the change pleasant, using the following years to write my research and for personal and family projects such as choral music, American musical theater, other interests, a family history, and memoirs of trips abroad. My latest book concerned a male chorus that I directed a number of years ago at the University of North Dakota [Author's note: I was a member of that chorus] initiated by my 83rd birthday, when 40 of my old Varsity Bard members showed up to help me celebrate. Thereafter I decided to write a memoir of those days plus the insertion of a CD of some of our performances. In this fashion, I have not experienced regret for letting go. I should say that I have substituted a number of times for younger colleagues who have taken sabbaticals from their respective campuses and have been involved in a number of church choirs over the years.

"We had planned to retire in Grinnell and did. However, our son Tom got a job with the public radio station in San Diego, so my wife and I pulled up stakes and moved here in 2000 to be near family and to babysit. Life has been good."—James T. Fudge, PhD, Professor Emeritus, Grinnell College

SUMMARY

This chapter discussed maintaining good health before and after retirement. Special attention was paid to common health problems of older workaholic adults, including heart problems, adult-onset diabetes, and the loss of cognitive functioning related to Alzheimer's and other forms of brain disorders. Special attention was given to recognizing problems as they occur and then seeking out appropriate medical care. Two personal stories involving workaholics with health problems and the impact retirement has had on them were included.

SUGGESTED WEB SITES

Alzheimer's Association, http://www.alz.org/.
American Diabetes Association, http://www.diabetes.org/.
American Heart Association, http://www.americanheart.org/presenter.jhtml?
        identifier=1200000.
Senior Health (Medline Plus), http://www.nlm.nih.gov/medlineplus/seniors
        health.html.

REFERENCES

Aaron, F., Hughes, J., Buehler, J., Mittelmark, M., Jacobs, D., & Grimm, R. (1985).
        Do type A men drink more frequently than type B men? Findings in the

Multiple Risk Factor Intervention Trial (MRFIT). *Journal of Behavioral Medicine, 8,* 227–235.

Alzheimer's Association. (2009). *Alzheimer's facts and figures.* Retrieved February 16, 2010, from: http://www.alz.org/national/documents/report_alzfactsfigures 2009.pdf.

American Heart Association. (2008). *Heart attack and angina statistics.* Retrieved May 7, 2009, from http://www.americanheart.org/presenter.jhtml?iden tifier=4591.

Carle, A. (2007,February). More than a game: Brain training against dementia. *Nursing Home Magazine,* 22–24.

Colcombe, S., Erickson, K., Scalf, P., Kim, J., Prakash, R., McAuley, E., et al. (2006). Aerobic exercise training increases brain volume in aging humans. *Journals of Gerontology: Medical Sciences, 61A,* 1166–1170.

Courtenay, W.H. (1996). *Health mentor: Health risk assessment for men.* Berkeley, CA: Self-Published.

Courtenay, W.H. (2000). Behavioral factors associated with disease, injury, and death among men: Evidence and implications for prevention. *Journal of Men's Studies, 9,* 81–104.

Drug Store News. (1998, July 20). Men's health at a glance: A fact sheet for pharmacists. Retrieved May 17, 2004, from http://www.findarticles.com/cf_0/m3374/n11_v20/20969541/p1/article.jhtml?term=men+%2B+health.

Duke University Medical Center. (2008). *Aspirin in heart attack prevention: How much, how long?* Retrieved February 12, 2009, from http://www.dukemed news.org/news/article.php?id=10217.

George, L. (2007,April 9). The secret to not losing your marbles. *Macleans,* 36–39.

Gupta, S. (2003, May 12). Why men die young. *Time, 161*(19), 84.

Harrison, J., Chin, J., & Ficarrotto, T. (1988). Warning: Masculinity may be dangerous to your health. In M.S. Kimmel & M.A. Messner (Eds.), *Men's lives* (pp. 271–285). New York: Macmillan.

Karlberg, L., Unden, A.-L., Elofsson, S., & Krakau, I. (1998, Fall). Is there a connection between car accidents, near accidents, and type A drivers? *Behavioral Medicine, 16,* 207–219.

Lunde, A. (2008, March 24). *Preventing Alzheimer's: Exercise still best bet.* Retrieved August 12, 2009, from http://www.mayoclinic.com/health/alzheimers/MY00002.

Mayo Clinic. (2008). *Preventing heart attacks.* Retrieved August 12, 2009, from http://www.mayoclinic.com/health/heart-attack/DS00094/DSECTION=pre vention.

National Institute for Occupational Safety and Health. (1993). *Fatal injuries to workers in the United States, 1980–1989: A decade of surveillance* (DHHS Report No. 93-108). Cincinnati, OH: Author.

Pedraza, J.M. (2008, June).Preventing Alzheimers: Is coffee the answer?. *Dimensions: The University of North Dakota, 2.*

Saunders, C.S. (2000). Where are all the men? *Patient Care, 16*(4), 12–18.

Scarmeas, N., Stern, Y., Tang, M.-X., Mayeux, R., & Luchsinger, J. (2006). Mediterranean diet lowers Alzheimer's risk in American cohort. *Annals of Neurology.* Retrieved May 2, 2009, from http://www.eurekalert.org/pub_releases/2006-04/jws-mdl041106.php.

Vaillant, G.E. (2002). *Aging Well.* New York : Little, Brown and Company.

Vaillant, G. E., & Mukamal, K. (2001). Successful aging. *American Journal of Psychiatry, 158*(6), 839–847.

Wilson, R. S., Schneider, J. A., Arnold, S. E., Bienias, J. L., & Bennett, D. A. (2007). Conscientiousness and the incidence of Alzheimer disease and cognitive impairment. *Archives of General Psychiatry, 64*, 1204–1212.

PART V

After Retirement: Repairing Personal Relationships with Family and Loved Ones

Chapters 13 and 14 discuss repairing relationships with loved ones, family members, and friends. The ability to repair these close personal relationships after years of conflict or abandonment in favor of work can make retirement and the work you do after retirement much more fulfilling and personally gratifying. Repairing close intimate relationships also provides a support group, an important aspect of retirement satisfaction and a safety net in times of crisis.

CHAPTER 13

Repairing Intimate Relationships

Many workaholic readers have probably made something of a mess of their personal lives. Putting off intimacy and a close family life in favor of work has a way of pushing away the people you love. By the time you are ready for retirement, you may be looking at some very lonely times without loving people in your life. What can you do at this point to bring love and intimacy into your life and enjoy the benefits of close personal relationships? For the reader who wants to repair an existing marriage and long-term relationships that have suffered from years of neglect because of overwork, or for the reader who wants to start over again, this chapter is about mature love.

MATURE LOVE

Older adults experience love in a more accepting and emotionally healthy way than younger people. Older love is often more patient. Zernike (2007) notes that for older adults, "as we experience the good and bad times, they're more precious, they're richer" (p. 1). It may also be true that older people are simply better able to deal with the emotional aspects of love. According to brain researchers, as the brain ages, it becomes more programmed to be happy in relationships. Zernike adds,

As people get older, they seem to naturally look at the world through positivity and be willing to accept things that when we're young we would find disturbing and vexing. It is not rationalization: the reaction is instantaneous. Instead of what would be most disturbing for somebody, feeling betrayed or discomfort, the other thoughts—about how from his perspective it's not betrayal—can be accommodated much more easily, it paves the way for you to be sympathetic to the situation from his perspective, to be less disturbed from her perspective. (2)

Walsh (1988) believes that married older couples often experience increased marital satisfaction and intimacy as they begin to realize that they have only limited time left to be a couple. Of course, there are also older adults who maintain troubled approaches to love and "who are just as jealous, just as infantile, just as filled with irrationality when they fall in love in their 70s and 80s as [they were at earlier ages]. And it still is possible to have a broken heart in old age. A broken heart looks different in somebody old. You don't yell and scream like you might when you were 20" (Zernike, 2007, 3).

Barusch (2009) interviewed a number of people aged 51 to 97 and found that those who were married or in a committed relationship reported that love consistently improved with age. The author also found that people over 50 in new relationships reported higher romantic, physical, and emotional intensity than younger adults in new relationships. The author reported that the definition of love changed as people aged and included caretaking and less restricted gender roles. Men in particular craved additional intimacy as they aged. Intimacy issues in the author's study were broadly defined to include erotic love for some and chastity for others. Many of the people in her study were content with touching and hugs and other indicators of affection.

Khaleque (2003) found that intimate adult relationships are one of the most important predictors of psychological adjustment in later life. Khaleque also suggests that past research has found that disruptions in early-childhood attachments to parents may affect the quality of intimate relationships in later life. Rohner and Khaleque (2003) found that childhood experiences of parental acceptance and rejection have significant influence on partner acceptance and rejection, and even in later life, we often choose intimate partners based on the patterns of acceptance and rejection by parents that we experienced in childhood. Because we often outgrow these early patterns in those with whom we seek to have intimacy, it may help explain why older love differs from younger love in that we seek people who are more truly our *Beshert*, our chosen ones.

OLDER LOVE AND INTIMACY

Regarding older adult intimacy, Stein (2007) reports the results of a study of 3,000 U.S. adults aged 57 to 85. The study found that half to three-quarters of the respondents remained sexually active, with a "significant population engaging in frequent and varied sex" (p. A1). The study found that physically healthier people reported the highest rates of sexual activity and that a healthy sex life may itself keep people vibrant. According to Stein, the study noted that 28 percent of the men and 14 percent of the women said sex was very important, and those with partners reported being sexually active as often as people in their 40s and 50s. "But even among the oldest age group (80–85), 54% of those who were sexually active reported having sex at least two to three times per month and 23% reported having sex once a week or more" (4).

Infatuation   Most of us think of infatuation as a prelude to love, but a number of authors and researchers view infatuation as a negative emotional experience. For example, Drew (2009) defines *infatuation* as "a static process characterized by an unrealistic expectation of blissful passion without positive growth and development. Characterized by a lack of trust, lack of loyalty, lack of commitment, lack of reciprocity, an infatuation is not necessarily foreplay for a love scenario" (3). Peach (2009) writes that infatuation is often called being "a fool in love" and is usually seen as "a state in which a person's normal ability to think clearly and act rationally are [*sic*] flung aside with suspicious eagerness. Desire focuses on a particular someone and suddenly nothing matters but that compelling attraction" (2).

In discussing the difference between love and infatuation, Drew (2009) suggests that with infatuation, the faults you refused to see when the relationship was new will became obvious, but with love, "our focus is on your special someone, and that someone exists in the real world. Give and take, compromise and cooperation are characteristics of love relationships. Working toward common goals, sharing dreams and values define the dynamics of a good love relationship. People know each other on a separate and private level than the world at large" (6).

Barusch (2009) believes that American culture puts a great deal of weight on infatuation, often giving it a major role in the way we think about romance. We often believe that infatuation is the initial experience we feel that will result in a long-term commitment. Although most older adults know that infatuation is a temporary state, it's easy to forget that when you're in its grip. Barusch writes about a client in his late 50s who planned to leave his wife of 30 years for a new love:

Over a period of several months, he spoke for hours at a time about this infatuation. Later, he told me I had saved his marriage with one statement. As he fantasized about life with his beloved, I asked about his children, wondering whether his new love would be as interested in his children as their mother and how that might play out when grandchildren came along. He felt this conversation was a tipping point, setting the stage for the infatuation's slow fade. Eventually, he was able to rededicate himself to the marriage. (p. 12)

A PERSONAL VIEW OF MATURE LOVE

The following excerpt comes from my new book on mature love and expresses my definition of older adult love (Glicken, in press).

When I think of mature love, I think of two people who feel comfortable with one another. They can talk, plan, touch, be intimate, and carry positive feelings for each other through disagreements and times of stress. They protect one another from the fear of being alone and without anyone there in a health crisis. They know our emotional blind spots and accept us for who we are, not who they wish we were. They are grounded in the present. Instead of bringing up old experiences that involved other people, they focus on the here and now. They don't make unrealistic demands on each other but use gentle persuasion to help their partners see blind spots that may sometimes interfere in the relationship.

When times are tough in the relationship, as they sometimes are, people in a mature relationship play fair. They don't use tactics that hurt the relationship irreparably just for the sake of winning. They think of themselves as "us" rather than "me and you." They appreciate the talents and abilities of their partners and encourage and support growth. In a mature relationship, there are no stars but instead two partners who work and play together, rather than two disparate people living their own lives.

Mature love means equality. It means that although one person may do better in certain areas of the relationship or have special skills, when everything is tallied, the contribution to the relationship is equal. Mature love means that time is spent understanding the special abilities of each partner so that those abilities serve to strengthen the relationship. Mature love means never using sarcasm or embarrassing a partner in public. And unlike *Love Story*, mature love means saying you're sorry every five minutes, if necessary. In a mature relationship, apologizing should come easily, and it should always come from the heart.

If you've had children by someone other than your partner, mature love means treating the children of your partner as if they were yours—with love, tenderness, and concern. It means never criticizing your partner's children because it's hurtful, and there are better ways to share your feelings. Mature love means understanding that you and your partner have the need to be alone with your own children and that giving your partner the time and space to be together, even if it means a week or more without your partner, is part of the responsibility of being older adults in a loving and tender relationship.

Mature love means that you are both involved in keeping the relationship vital and interesting. This doesn't mean that you have to hop around the world or be on the go all the time. It means that relationships become stale in time if two people aren't equally involved in activities that are fun, challenging, and memorable. The mate who always plans while her partner goes along is not taking responsibility for keeping the relationship alive. Passive people add nothing to relationships.

Mature love means that you plan to be with your partner through sickness and ill health—no fudging on this one. Mature love means that you've anticipated the many things that can happen to older people and that you've made a commitment to them and to yourself—a sacred vow, really—that no matter what, you'll be there for them, through sickness and health, 'til death do you part. Otherwise, you're just playing at love, and you have an exit strategy. That isn't mature love; it's adolescent love. It's the type of love that results in breakups, divorces, hurt feelings, and broken hearts. It has no place in the world of mature love. Unless you make a pledge to your loved one that you'll be there for him, no matter what, you can't call your relationship mature or loving. If you have an exit strategy, you should call it what it is: temporary, uncommitted, and separate.

Mature love is based in reality. Most of us after a certain age don't walk along the beach hand in hand watching the sunset and then have drinks over a candlelit dinner before making love while listening to the waves break. Sometimes we do, of course, but we can't do that every night or think of love as something out of a bad romance novel. Unfortunately, many older people have that view of love. When a relationship doesn't last because of unrealistic expectations, the view either doesn't change or becomes cynical. Mature love is based on deep feelings of affection and warmth, not walks along the beach. I think most of us know that, but unfortunately, too many older people base their notions of love and romance on the popular culture rather than the wisdom of older men and women whose relationships have lasted and prospered.

Most of all, mature love means that you can become old together and not worry about your loved one becoming emotionally and physically detached because she no longer finds you interesting or attractive. Mature people recognize that aging is an equal opportunity employer: as you age and want your loved one to continue finding you attractive, your partner has the same need. Flirting, carrying on relationships behind your mate's back, or having secret friendships is hurtful and just not part of a mature relationship. There are rules of civility that apply in mature love. If you can't accept the rules and you still think of yourself as an older adolescent, you will not be able to call a relationship mature or loving.

SUMMARY

This chapter discussed mature love and the differences between infatuation, love with an exit strategy, and mature love. Mature love is love that grows slowly and builds into a positive, long-term, honest, and loyal adult love. Infatuation is the high many of us experience when we first meet someone who totally involves us but begins to wither as we get to know that person better and see the flaws that make mature love unlikely. Love with an exit strategy is love with limits. Older work-addicted people should be particularly suspicious of infatuation and the negative consequences of falling in love too quickly. Mature love takes time to develop and with any addiction, falling in love with someone who also has a work addiction can be very troublesome.

REFERENCES

Bancroft, J.H.J. (2007). *Sex and aging*. Retrieved July 7, 2009, from, http://cas.umkc.edu/casww/sa/Sex.htm.

Barusch, A.S. (2009). Love and ageism—A social work perspective. *Social Work Today, 9*(1), 12.

Clinical Effectiveness Group. (2005). *National guidelines for the management of the viral hepatitides A, B and C*. Retrieved October 8, 2008, from http://www.bashh.org/guidelines/2005/hepatitis.

Drew, M. (2009). *Love vs. infatuation*. Retrieved June 23, 2009, from http://www.mental-health-matters.com/articles/article.php?artID=853.

Genevay, B. (1999). Intimacy and older people: Much more than sex. *Dimensions, 6*(3), 6–12.

Glicken, M.D. (in press). *Mature friendships, love, and romance: A practical guide to intimacy for older adults*. Santa Barbara, CA: Praeger.

Khaleque, A. (2003). Intimate adult relationships, quality of life and psychological adjustment. *Social Indicators Research, 69*, 351–360.

National Council on the Aging. (1998, September). *Healthy sexuality and vital aging* (Executive Summary) Washington, D.C: Author.

Peach, D. (2009). *Infatuation*. Retrieved February 6, 2009, from http://www.sosuave.com/articles/infatuation.htm.

Rohner, R.P., & Khaleque, A. (2003). *Relations between partner acceptance and parental acceptance, behavioral control, and psychosocial adjustment among heterosexual adult women*. Unpublished manuscript, 1–14.

Stein, R. (2007, August 23). Elderly staying sexually active. *Washington Post*. Retrieved July 7, 2009, from http://www.washingtonpost.com/wp-dyn/content/article/2007/08/22/AR2007082202000_pf.html.

Walsh, F. (1988). The family in later life. In B. Carter & M. McGoldrick (Eds.), *The changing family life cycle* (2nd ed., pp. 311–332). New York: Gardner.

Zernike, K. (2007, November 18). Still many-splendored: Love in the time of dementia. *New York* Times. Retrieved August 17, 2009, from http://www.nytimes.com/2007/11/18/weekinreview/18zernike.html.

CHAPTER 14

Repairing Relationships with Family and Friends

FRIENDSHIPS

We humans are social beings, and without social contacts, most of us become lonely and depressed. One source of social contacts is friends, and though many work-addicted people can claim few real friends as they move into retirement, it's not too late to start making some.

We all know that having friends in our lives, good friends, is a blessing as we age. Friends are those trusting, loyal people who are there for us in a crisis and remain loyal even when there are conflicts between us. Acquaintances are people in our lives who don't have the same level of loyalty. They come and go, and we usually don't think of them as close friends. Unfortunately, we often confuse acquaintances with friends, and this sometimes leads to unhappiness.

When the elements of good friendship were evaluated by age, Schnittker (2007) found that older adults expect "agreeableness" in their friends, or the ability to get along. Not surprisingly, the researcher also found that we base our concept of friendship on the early messages given to us by parents about our friends. Favorable feedback about friends at an early age can have a lasting impact on who we consider to be friendship material.

According to Paul (2005), new research suggests that friendships profoundly impact our physical and emotional health by boosting the immune system, offering protection from anxiety and depression, and improving memory as well as the ability to sleep well. She goes on to say that although men need friendships, they often turn to their wives for many of the things friends do, largely because women tend to be more soothing and comforting in relationships. She points out that one study found that when women and men were placed in stressful situations, people who were placed with women had lower stress levels than people who were placed with men. She believes the reason this happened is because women are better listeners and are much less likely than men to try to fix things by giving unwanted advice. Whether this is true depends on your personal experience, but I've found women to be better listeners and more interested in details and concerns about intimate issues.

Chen (2009) notes that "many studies have shown the benefits of friendship on positive social, emotional, and physical well-being. Having a strong circle of friends can be a good source for aging hearts and help the body's autoimmune system resist disease. People who have one or more good friends have better health than those who have only causal friends or no friends" (p. 1). Chen also says that many older people live alone and lack even one good friend. She notes that in the United States, one out of every three women and one of every seven men aged 65 or older lives alone. She also finds that men have a harder time dealing with their widowhood than women. About two-thirds of older men reported that they did not have a close friend, while 16 percent of widows reported having no friends.

Regarding differences between men and women and the way they define friendships, Felmlee and Muraco (2009) found that women in later life stages placed more emphasis on intimacy in their friendships than men did and also had higher expectations of friends. The researchers found that women were "more disapproving of violations of friendship rules, such as betraying a confidence, paying a surprise visit, and failing to stand up for a friend in public" (p. 318). However, men and women share important notions of friendship that are based on trust, commitment, and respect. These general notions of friendship remain throughout the life span and are as true for younger people as they are for older adults.

Parents discuss issues of friendship with children and help us define the attributes of friendships. One single older adult I know said that his mother's favorite expression was "better a good friend nearby than a family member far away." What she meant was that we often rely on friends more than family. For our friend's mother, friendship was a serious commitment to others. In some ways, it was like being committed to a spouse because it implied high expectations. Needless to say, these high standards for friendship brought a good deal of grief to our friend, who told us that he'd been disappointed in people he thought were friends for as long as he could remember. It seems evident that our definition of friendship has a good deal to do with whether we are able to find and retain friends.

The following story by a 75-year-old single woman discusses the bittersweet experiences of forming and sometimes failing to find the good friendships most of us long for.

Personal Story: Friends

Friends

Three are my friends.
One who loves me.
One who hates me.
One who is indifferent to me.
Who loves me, teaches me tenderness.
Who hates me, teaches me caution.
Who is indifferent to me, teaches me self-reliance.

"There's an e-mail floating around in cyberspace that says, 'People come into your life for a reason, a season, or a lifetime.' When someone is in your life for a reason, it is usually to meet a need you have expressed. When someone comes in for a season, it's usually because your turn has come to share, grow, or learn. Lifetime relationships teach you lifetime lessons, things you must build upon in order to have a solid emotional foundation. Your job is to accept the lesson.

"When I was growing up, my friends and I all lived on the same block. We would play together all day and into the night during the summer when it stayed light out until late into the evening. Life was safe back then, and there were no monsters roaming the streets looking for innocent children.

"We played ball in a vacant lot, we jumped rope out front, tag was popular, as were marbles and jacks. There were flowers to smell, butterflies to catch, clouds to gaze into, and plates of cookies in every house. We all went to the same schools, and no one ever talked about what went on when we went home and the door was closed.

"The friends I made then have been coming back and forth into my life for the past 55 years, but wherever we end up, we always know that the connection of growing up together is still there.

"We see each other at high school reunions and catch up with what's been happening in our lives with notes in the alumni association's newsletter. We may not see each other for years, but when we do get together, it's as if we've never been apart.

"I've now discovered that of the people who have come into my life since then, most of them have only come into my life for a season, and I wonder if the word *acquaintance* wouldn't better describe them than *friend*. At times I would think that I had made a really good friend, only to discover months later that they had in reality only come into my life for a reason or a season. I can't count the number of times that I've asked myself, what did I do wrong? It took many years of inner dialogue to accept the fact that they were only there for a short time and that I had nothing to do with them leaving. And yes, there were lessons I had to learn and pain I had to overcome. Of the lessons they were supposed to teach me, I hope I've learned them all.

"By nature I'm normally a shy person when it comes to meeting new people, and that's required some work through the years, too. Now I can talk to anyone, anyplace, anytime, but I still find myself holding back a little when it comes to making a friendship. You know how it goes. You talk to someone, find out what their interests are until you find something common to share with him. It either takes off from there or dies at the end of the conversation. I've met people that thought the same as I did on a number of subjects, but we could never be friends, the chemistry just wasn't there. And then there have been some that I would have given my eldest child to be friends with, but I wasn't worth the effort to them.

"And so it's gone through the years. I have friends from childhood that I communicate with on a regular basis, I have friends that I attended school with, I have friends that I sing with and friends that I can just hang around with. But in the final analysis, there are three women that would be at my side, without question, should I need them: one who I shared a Bat Mitzvah with 25 years ago, that's Linda; one that shares my passions, that's Theresa; and the last is my youngest daughter, Rosalie, who holds me up when I falter and convinces me to keep on going.

"I lost a friend on July 4 of this year. We buried Sharon last Sunday. I looked around at the group of people at her grave site and realized along with her family and neighbors that there were longtime friends and that we had all added something different to her life, as she had to ours.

"Our rabbi read letters that had been written by members of her family, all recalling something that was special to each to them. It was very moving, and I realized that while it's very important to have friends around when you're alive and crave laughter and company, it's also good to have them after you're gone. They're the ones who will smile when your name is mentioned and tell everyone within listening distance what you meant to them. They keep you alive long after your spirit has left. It's like a quote that I once read by an anonymous writer: 'without friends you're like a book that nobody bothers to pick up.'"—Gladys Smith, Long Beach, California

FAMILIES

One of the more hurtful experiences older adults tell me about is the less-than-successful relationships they have with children and other family members. They talk of an eroding amount of contact, lack of cards or calls on birthdays, attempts to get closer or resolve problems that are ignored, and a feeling that children and brothers and sisters they loved so much early in life have turned away from them for reasons they can't understand. In this section of the chapter, we'll look at research on family interactions, and I'll make suggestions about how you can improve relationships—suggestions that come from my own experience as a social worker, teacher, father, and brother of two siblings. But before I do that, let's look at some of the research on family interactions with older adults.

Although many of us believe that children and family members will let us down as we age, particularly when we are most in need of their involvement, Glaser, Stuchbury, Tomasine, and Askham (2008) found that to the contrary, children often help out when older adult marriages dissolve or in the event of the death of a spouse. The researchers also found that although much of the current literature points to a distancing by family members if an older adult divorces, the researchers found a changing attitude toward the divorcing parent who remarries, and as much help is given when needed to that parent as when she was still married to a long-term mate.

What we *do* know is that some older adults have had troubled relationships with their children over a long period of time. This is particularly true of parents who were emotionally aloof, failed to form an attachment because of long periods of time away from their children, abused alcohol and drugs, or were physically and emotionally abusive. To think that these children will form positive attachments with their older adult parents and provide supportive help when it's needed may be unrealistic. Shu (2005) reports that almost two-thirds (67%) of all elder abuse is committed by adult children and their spouses. Before plans are made to heavily involve yourself with adult children and their families, you really need to evaluate the quality of your relationship with your children. If there have been unresolved problems in the past that continue on, not a few of us have sought professional help to try to find new ways of dealing with our children.

In her book *Walking on Eggshells: Navigating the Delicate Relationship between Adult Children and Their Parents,* Isay (2008) interviewed dozens of older adult parents and their adult children about resolving tensions and improving communications. The title refers to the fact that the people she interviewed felt as if they were walking on eggshells with one another and felt fearful that saying or doing the wrong thing would disturb fragile relationships. These are her suggestions:

1. Try to understand the personal communication styles of everyone in your family. Don't think that everyone has the same way of communicating, and don't let spouses or friends interfere with those communication styles if they are working. What works for them may not work for you.

2. Have the important discussions about finances, wills, and advance directives with all your children present. Don't play favorites and just talk to the child you think will give the best advice or is the easiest to talk to. That's a sure way to alienate your other children who weren't part of the process. When everyone is together, decisions are made using the knowledge of everyone present rather than a few children who may not represent the entire family. It might surprise you how much your children know about finances or the wise suggestions they give.

3. Although it's often best to talk on the phone or see your loved ones in person, the important thing is to stay in touch. I use e-mail a lot, but my daughter and I talk on the phone every week about the more important things that e-mail doesn't quite permit. We're both computer people, and e-mail is a quick

and easy way for us to stay in touch. If we have other things that need talking about, we use e-mail to decide the best time to talk. Deciding in advance on times to talk or to meet recognizes that my daughter is far busier than I am and can't always talk when it's convenient for me.

4. Treat your loved ones with respect. Perhaps that's a cliché, but when I talk to my daughter, I recognize that she's a highly intelligent, highly competent adult with ideas and thoughts that are always interesting to hear. She also knows a lot more about a number of technical things than I do. I always try to be respectful and appreciative of the time we spend together. Next week, on a Sunday when she's free, we're meeting halfway between our homes and having lunch together. It allows us to see each other but avoids an extra two-hour drive. We try to do that a lot. I'm always amazed by how much she knows about things I know nothing about, and I'm always appreciative of the time she takes away from her busy life to be with me. I don't want these get-togethers to feel obligatory; rather, I'd like them to come naturally, as they usually do whenever we discuss meeting.

5. Be involved, but not to the point of suffocating your children. Big problems occur when either party begins to meddle in the other's lifestyle and decisions. Be involved, but not enmeshed. If the relationship is solid, children will ask for your advice. I've been a social worker all my professional life. People seldom if ever use advice that isn't asked for. In fact, they often resent it. I know I do, so I don't give advice. I offer suggestions when they are asked for. I've learned from my teaching career that everyone needs room to fail and that my job is to be supportive and encouraging. If students don't want to use my suggestions and fail, that's their right. It's not my job to save people from making mistakes. Instead, it's my job to help them learn from their mistakes if they ask for assistance.

Personal Story: Friends and Family

Jack is an 86-year-old tennis player and raconteur. He graciously let me interview him, and though the following aren't always his exact words, I've tried to be faithful to what he said. I wish to thank Elsevier for permission to reprint this story, which originally appeared in Glicken (2009). (This excerpt was published in *Evidence-Based Counseling and Psychotherapy with an Aging Population* by Morley D. Glicken, pp. 64–65, Copyright © Elsevier, 2009. Reprinted with permission.)

"Until I remarried and began a successful business in my mid-50s, I guess you could say that I had no point of view and did what I thought other people wanted me to do. The change took place while I was looking at a property to buy in East Los Angeles, and I was shot and seriously wounded in a random shooting. The bullet took out part of my liver. It took me six months to get over the shock and the physical pain.

"During the time I was recuperating, my wife and I decided to move to Hawaii and start a new business. I had very little money, and we knew we were taking a chance, but in the 10 years we worked at building our business, we were able to plan for our eventual retirement, sell our business at a nice profit, and find this community in paradise. [He points to the pines and the mountains nearby. We're sitting outside watching a tennis match and talking, and it's a perfect day, sunny and warm, with the smell of spring in the Arizona high country.]

"I surround myself with people who are optimistic and make me laugh. I think laughter is the healthiest emotion, and even though I have some serious health problems, I take care of myself and I don't dwell on them. I know my tennis is limited and that there are many things I can't do anymore, but getting out with a bunch of guys, hitting the ball, and then going out for coffee and laughing together—it's the best thing about my life.

"My wife is someone who takes care of me when I need it and who helped me develop our business that ultimately allowed us to retire and enjoy life. My first wife was someone who always had us in debt and who I think never loved me or felt anything about me, except that I was a provider. My current wife and I met while we were developing a new synagogue in Los Angeles. We had time to get to know each other and to appreciate how many things we had in common and how well we got along.

"One of our sons was gay and died of AIDS. He had a doctor-assisted suicide in Oregon, and it was very powerful. He had close friends over, and the minister of his church said some words about his life that still make me cry when I think about them. [He pauses and wipes tears from his eyes. I know that death isn't beautiful, but in its own way, it was. Since then, I've never feared dying. It took a while to get over his death, but I think about the joy he gave me when he was alive and well. I have another son we help out financially who's a graphic designer and talented but not very good with money.

"When I die, we'll be worth a lot of money, and I guess the family will get it. I think about spending it all now, but my needs are few and the traveling I wanted to do when I was younger we've already done. My wife had a hip replacement, and she'd rather stay at home anyway. It's fine with me.

"I don't think of myself as being religious. The guys joke about my being Jewish, but I'm just like them in most ways. While I'm proud of being a Jew, the religion never mattered much to me, just as their religions don't matter much to them. I was raised in a religious home, but it didn't stick.

"I have many friends, and I know that I could count on them if I needed their help. That's the best thing about life now, being able to be with people I like and who I think genuinely like me. I stay away from people who seem unhappy, and I know I flirt a lot with young women and say things to ladies at the tennis club most guys couldn't get away with. What the hell, I can't do anything about it anyway, and they know it, so why not? It's one of the privileges of being old. You can say things that would be offensive if you were younger, and everyone thinks it's charming now.

"I began mentoring a young boy in the first grade who was having some behavioral problems after his parents divorced. One of my friend's wives suggested that I'd be a good mentor for a young child, so I volunteered at the public school, and he was assigned to me. We hung out together, and I gave him a little support and encouragement. He's a senior in high school now and a colonel in the Civilian Air Patrol. I'm really proud of him. I think I did a better job with him than with my own sons, but then you get wiser as you age. Maybe I was good all along, but I felt more confident and comfortable with myself as I got older so that I could be a good friend instead of a parent.

"I started to become a real human being in my 50s, and it's just gotten better and better. I would say to anyone reading your book that you should make the most of your time and enjoy yourself. There's so little time to live that you should do it to the fullest. More than half my life was spent being unhappy, in debt, and feeling unloved. This opportunity I've had since I met my present wife has been a blessing, and we should all be open to change and to the possibilities of life. Good friends, laughter, enough money to be comfortable, and good health. That's all anyone can ask for when they're 86."—Jack Schwartz, Prescott, Arizona

SUMMARY

This chapter was about the differences between the true friends many of us long for and the more superficial acquaintances we have in our life, and how to tell the difference between the two. The chapter included a story by a 75-year-old woman on friendship and an 86-year-old man on the importance of friends and family. Our definition of *friendship* is often influenced by how our parents approached our friends when we were children and how they modeled friendships in their own lives.

The chapter also discussed reconciling with your family, particularly with your adult children. Suggestions were given to improve communication and to deal with the problem of trying to develop a good relationship with children after years of neglect.

REFERENCES

Cacioppo, J.T., & Patrick, B. (2008). *Loneliness: Human nature and the need for social connection*. New York: W.W. Norton & Company.

Chen, N. (2009). *Friendship is important to older adults*. Retrieved June 4, 2009, from http://missourifamilies.org/features/agingarticles/agingfeature11.htm.

Felmlee, D., & Muraco, A. (2009). Gender and friendship norms among older adults. *Research on Aging, 31*, 318–344.

Glaser, K., Stuchbury, R., Tomasine, C., & Askham, J. (2008). The long-term consequences of partnership dissolution for support in later life in the United Kingdom. *Aging and Society, 23*, 329–351.

Glicken, M.D. (2009). *Evidence-based counseling and psychotherapy with an aging population*. London: Elsevier.

Isay, J. (2008). *Walking on eggshells: Navigating the delicate relationship between adult children and their parents*. New York: Flying Dolphin Press.

Paul, M. (2005). *The friendship crisis: Finding, making, and keeping friends when you're not a kid anymore.* New York: Rondale Books.

Schnittker, J. (2007). Look (closely) at all the lonely people: Age and the social psychology of social support. *Journal of Aging and Health, 19,* 659–682.

Shu, E. (2005). Elder of dependent adult abuse. *Psychology Today.* Retrieved August 7, 2009, from http://www.psychologytoday.com/conditions/elder-or-dependent-adult-abuse.

PART VI

After Retirement: Work Opportunities and Dealing with Leisure Time

Chapter 15 discusses ways to stay occupied after retirement and the reasons workaholics have such trouble with leisure time. The chapter includes personal stories and examples from retired work-addicted people.

CHAPTER 15

Cycling Back to Work and Dealing with Leisure Time

Is it a good idea to cycle back to work once you're retired? And equally as important, if you do return to work, will your workaholic tendencies come back? Schneider (1998) points out that many Americans are workaholics and that when work is taken away or jobs are diminished in complexity and creativity, many older adults experience a decrease in physical and mental health.

Writing about the loss of work and its impact on older men, Levant (1997) says that as men lose their good-provider roles, the experience often results in "severe gender role strain" (p. 221) that affects relationships and can be disruptive to the point of ending otherwise strong marriages. Because older adults are more likely to lose high-level jobs because of downsizing and negative attitudes toward older workers, social contacts decrease, and many otherwise healthy and motivated workers must deal with increased levels of isolation and loneliness.

Heller (1993) reports that the loss of status and social roles when older adults no longer work can be devastating. He notes that "a major problem is that individuals lose institutional roles with age (e.g., forced retirement at age 65) and find that their contribution to society is devalued, not on the basis of personal attributes or behavior but because age has moved them to the role of a non-participant in society" (p. 125).

For many healthy, work-oriented, and motivated older adults, volunteer and civic roles are not what they are looking for. They want to continue to work, to contribute, and to receive the status and benefits related to work. But continued work beyond retirement age has negative implications for workers who have worked at physically and emotionally demanding jobs that have taken their toll on bodies and minds. This is particularly true of workaholics, who may have a strong desire to continue working at demanding jobs but no longer enjoy good physical or emotional health. Realistically, they can't work at the jobs that make them most satisfied and instead have to find creative outlets for work that are interesting and fulfilling but not physically or emotionally demanding.

IDEAS FOR WORK AFTER RETIREMENT

1. *Part-time work can be fulfilling and a lot less stressful.* At the end of the chapter, I've written a piece about my own experiences with work after retirement. When I retired, I knew I would never work full-time again. Why? Because I was pretty burned out. American universities have become very bureaucratic. Instead of the freewheeling places they used to be when I became an academic in the late 1960s, universities have become very rule driven and politically correct. If you fail a student, you know it invites a grade grievance you'll probably lose even if the student deserves the failing grade.

   I consider myself politically progressive, but political correctness and some really absurd ideas about student self-esteem if you fail them make what we do often seem self-defeating. And the salaries are nowhere near what one could make in the private for-profit area. In fact, one of the reasons I was burned out is that low salaries forced me to teach summers and do many weekend workshops, which didn't allow me breaks to renew myself or do the creative thinking one needs to do in university work.

   So what once felt important and noble felt odorous and inconsequential to me at 62. I'd saved enough money to retire, but what was good and productive about me hadn't been tapped in the university setting, and for the next few years, I searched for something else to do. I consulted (more on that next), wrote books, did workshops, and anything else I could think of to keep myself busy. Leisure time was my enemy. I didn't like it, I didn't know what to do about it, and I would rather work than play golf (my idea of a complete waste of time—sorry for that, you folks who are golfers).

   It takes time to find your way, but the personal story at the end of the chapter should help you understand that once you find a situation that gives you pleasure, a few days of work a week can make all the difference. Instead of working in university administration, as I had done for a number of years before I retired, I returned to teaching. I didn't know or care about the politics of the university. I came in, did my work, and focused on the students, many of whom were a gift. I put my heart into teaching and found that learning the new teaching technologies was a lot of fun. I learned to do audio PowerPoint presentations when I couldn't make class, thanks to a patient information technology person at the university. Ten years ago, I couldn't type, let alone use a computer. Today computers are my lifeline.

   It took me a year after I retired to get over being burned out and a few more to find a place to live where I liked being, but it's possible. So try part-time work, but remember that being a workaholic at a part-time job isn't what it's about. Part-time means you can have fun with the work. It doesn't have to be done right this minute, and you can think a bit about it. If it's too much, you can always quit, and nobody—and I mean nobody—will think badly of you for doing it . . . least of all you.

2. *Consulting.* Ernie Anderson is a 65-year-old engineer who lost his job in the global recession of 2008. He told me that when he and his wife sold their home, they had to find a place to live where the housing was inexpensive. Ernie had been treated for prostate cancer five years earlier and met a number of people who became his support group. One of them told Ernie that Sarasota, Florida, was a great place to live. I'll let Ernie tell the rest of his story:

"I loved my job. Everyday I went to work, I was happy to be there. I was certainly a workaholic, but it was out of love, not out of being neurotic. I just loved the hell out of my job. When our company went bankrupt, it almost broke my heart. We had to sell our house in suburban Chicago and, on the advice of a friend I'd met during my proton treatment at Loma Linda Hospital in California, I moved to a little town outside Sarasota and tried to find work. Impossible. He suggested that I join some local boards and see if that would lead to something. I joined the board of a local hospital. One day the board asked me if I would give a short talk about how an engineer would approach health care reform. When I found out about my cancer, I read some articles that Andy Grove, the cofounder of Intel and an engineer, wrote about how messed up the treatment of cancer was in America. Using that as a beginning, I told the group how engineers analyze problems and how it could benefit the health care field. Out of that little presentation, I was asked to consult with a small group of people to make the hospital more efficient and cost-effective. Like a number of hospitals, they were doing badly. We worked about a year. I received a small stipend, but out of that experience I was able to develop a consulting business for other hospitals and medical facilities in Florida. It keeps me busy, and the extra money is nice.

"I would say that if the same thing happens to you, use your contacts to find out about the volunteer organizations that can utilize your abilities. I also asked our real estate agent about the people in the community who could help me stay busy and joined several other boards. The work was interesting, and I felt connected and valued. With the housing market pretty much in shambles in Florida, we were able to sell our initial home and move to the beach, where we have a terrific, affordable condo with great ocean views. Sure, I'd rather be back in Chicago at my old job, but for a 65-year-old guy without a job a year ago, I think I've done well. Consulting from home gives me just enough work to stay busy and just enough leisure time to get the hang of what else to do with myself. I like to fish and sail. Who would have guessed? And I really like golf, a game I thought was about as dumb as they get. I've met some great people, and my wife and I have a busy social life, a lot busier than when we were in Chicago and all I had time for was work."

3. *Second Careers.* James Hanley is a 68-year-old former probation officer from Dubuque, Iowa, who retired at 66 when he began receiving his full Social Security and state pensions. He told me, "I had enough money to live on and didn't want to be a probation officer a second longer. Working with felons is one of the least rewarding things anyone can do. There isn't one who doesn't

try to con you, and they can drive you nuts because they're so manipulative. But I never got the hang of leisure time, and being single, I put all my energy into work, and then it stopped cold. I didn't know what to do with myself. It was driving me nuts.

"I'd always liked the idea of having a business, and I'm pretty handy with tools and I know a lot about fixing things. I'd been fixing friends' plumbing and electrical stuff for years, and it dawned on me that I could make a go of it as a business, so I got bonded and licensed and began letting people know I was available—sort of word of mouth. The work started coming in, and before I knew it, I had more than I could handle. The same people I'd helped kept calling me back. I charged about a third of what a plumber or electrician would charge and never did big things, just handyman work.

"In the meantime, I sort of got interested in making furniture and decided that four hours a day of handyman work was plenty, and the rest of the time I could use to build furniture, which I sold and made some very good money. One of my customers, a very nice lady and I began to date, and we're talking about getting married. For an old bachelor, that's a big step, but it feels right.

"One thing I should add is that I have a friend who's a pretty wise person and helps people find their work interests. I went to him and he pointed out that doing handyman work was natural and something people needed. Sometimes you need help in seeing the obvious. He helped me find out about bonding and licensure, and he helped me advertise and market both my handyman and furniture-making businesses. He also hooked me in with artisans who sell their work at fairs and arts and crafts shows. So Lila and I go somewhere new once a month to sell my stuff. It's fun meeting people, and right now I'm back ordered six months for furniture people want me to make. I may do furniture making full-time now, but the handyman work is fun, and people I work with never try to con me and appreciate the heck out of what I do. A number of them say that I'm part of their families."

4. *Going Back to School.* Alice Bennett is a 64-year-old lawyer from Denver, Colorado, whose bankruptcy law firm was disbanded several years earlier after the passage of a new federal bankruptcy law. Alice told me, "I was pretty fed up with the law by then, and I had saved enough money to retire, but you don't go from working 80 hours a week to full retirement. It took me a while to get my bearings and to see a career psychologist, who did some testing and also had some pretty smart things to suggest. Turns out I love the outdoors, but I also love literature. I wanted to get a master's degree in literature and maybe teach at a community college. The fellow I saw to help me with career choices told me about a summer job he thought I'd like—one that would help me work on my degree at the same time. I enrolled in a terrific online program at a major university and went to work for the forest service as a forest fire spotter.

"A fire spotter works alone in a tower looking for fires. I got so good at it that I could tell the intensity of the fire by the color, and I could almost pinpoint how far away it was. They put you in remote places and you work alone, which was fine with me. I loved the peace and quiet, and I could work on my degree at the same time. I worked in Oregon, California, and Washington during fire season. I spotted fires that could have damaged the forest, but they contained them before they became a problem. It was pretty wonderful work after the humdrum work I did as a lawyer.

"I got my master's degree, and I'm teaching English courses at our local community college. They asked me to teach a law course and to help them design a paralegal program. It's pretty great to be doing work where money isn't the main goal. The pay is enough for me to take some great summer hikes around the world during summer break. I do a little legal work, not much, and I'm thinking of maybe doing a doctorate in English and teaching at a four-year college. Being around students keeps me on my toes. I'm almost grateful the firm dissolved, or I wouldn't be doing what I'm doing now.

"I'd say to anyone who still wants to work that education is a great bargain in America. You'd be surprised how many older people you see on campus getting degrees or just taking courses because they're interested. If you want to develop a second career, getting new training is a great way to go."

DEALING WITH LEISURE TIME

One of the major problems that work-addicted retired people have is what to do with themselves. Work is often the most available answer, but then what do you do when you're not working? Plenty, but you need to do a little creative thinking. I like tennis. I've been playing it for years, and I usually play about eight hours a week, mostly in the mornings because the endorphins kick in from exercising and I can write for a few hours afterward. I like to read newspapers and books, but not at home, so I've found a great coffee shop in Prescott called the Wild Iris, where they know what I like to drink, make it just right, and have all the newspapers I want to read freely available. An hour there is a refreshing experience that allows me to write more when I get home. Maxie, my magical dog, and I try to do a weekly hike somewhere new in the Arizona mountains. I like to watch first-run films and belong to Netflix, which allows me to see films at home and not deal with the noise in movie theaters. It's also a lot cheaper. I like the free and not too expensive social and cultural activities in Prescott like the cowboy poetry festival, the blue grass and jazz festivals, and the Phoenix Symphony. There's a lot going on here and where you live as well. Read the local paper, find out what's going on, and start attending. Here's what a workaholic friend told me about leisure time:

I retired at 68 from running my own company. I'd say I was a workaholic. How can you run a company and not be? I'd begun to have heart problems and the doctor said to slow down or else, so we moved to Prescott, and suddenly I was faced with what to do with myself. I play golf and tennis, but it's just not enough, so I started to volunteer at Meals on Wheels, and I hated it. Not to say anything bad about that organization. They do good work. It's just that I'm a type A guy, and I know it. I was driving my wife batty hanging around the house. She said for me to start getting out of the house or she'd kill me.

So I read the local paper and found out there was plenty going on. I rejoined the Chamber of Commerce and Kiwanis because I belonged before I retired. I went to political debates and found I liked them. I got into a conversation with a young lady running for state office. She'd just started running and needed help, so I offered to help her with fund-raising and managing her campaign. She's a lot more liberal than I am, but she's a good person, and I trust her to do right for voters. I found out there were things going on in town that I wanted to speak out about. We're a water-poor area, and people are talking about diverting water from a local scenic river, but if we were to do that, we'd ruin the area by the river, which is—trust me—pretty darn nice. Why move to a place like this for its beauty and then ruin it? So I formed a committee to stop that from happening.

I started helping local businesses having difficulty as a volunteer, but that's sort of become a consulting business, and I meet a group of guys every other day to have coffee and kibitz. I go to the local concerts on the square with my wife, and we've begun seeing our kids more often and traveling. Suddenly I'm as busy as ever, and I'm happy, too.

What I'd tell anyone who doesn't know how to handle free time is to take advantage of what's going on. There's plenty happening. It's a tough time for our country, and we need the best people we can get in government. I feel that since I retired, I'm a better citizen. Things that bother me I speak out about, and I'm not shy to let people know what I believe when I'm asked. I ran a business, and that gives me plenty of knowledge about how things can work well if they're run right. My wife drags me on hikes. I hate it, but I admit it helps my heart, and the scenery is spectacular. I'm a rigid guy, I know it, but I feel some of that going away, and the person I'm becoming is a better person than the workaholic businessman I was before. But it's not easy to move from working full-time to taking it easy. Don't be too tough on yourself if it takes a while to get the hang of it.

WHY WORKAHOLICS HAVE SUCH TROUBLE WITH FREE TIME

There are a number of reasons why free time troubles workaholics. Here are a few:

1. *Workaholics have neglected to develop outside interests and hobbies and have no other interests than work.* This is pretty common, and the way to start dealing with it as you transition into retirement is to do an audit of what you really like to do. You may need to think back in time and do some soul searching to remember what you liked to do earlier in life, and then test it out to see if you still do.

2. *The hard-work mentality often devalues leisure time and outside interests.* It's a type of elitist attitude that says anything other than work is too beneath you to even to think about doing. You should know immediately that this is a pretty self-defeating notion because we all need to relax, and developing outside interests is a healthy way to reduce stress and add pleasure to your life.

3. *The belief that you'll try something once and if you don't like it, that's it.* Many of the things we ultimately like take time to develop an interest in. If you don't

like it a second or third time, OK, but give it at least another try. You may be surprised to find that your initial dislike goes away. Square dancing? Rap concerts? Maybe not, but there are other interesting things that might appeal to you if you give them a try.

4. *The notion that leisure time is sinful.* I mean it. There are people who think that if you're not busy every second of the time, you've committed a sin—or the workaholic equivalent of one. It's OK to goof off. It's OK to sit and watch TV or read a book. The world doesn't end, and you won't go to workaholic hell. Try it; you'll probably like it.

5. *Leisure time is the time to have happy hour.* There is nothing wrong with a drink or two, but equating leisure time with happy hour is something that could very well lead to abusive drinking. How about using happy hour to meet with interesting friends and keep to a strict limit on the number of drinks you have? Better yet, enjoy your friends and have a diet Coke. Now that sounds like fun, and you don't need to worry about the drive home.

6. *There just isn't anything to do that really interests me.* Come on now, nothing at all? That sounds like an excuse to me. Again, check your local newspaper for the weekly calendar. If there is nothing at all that interests you, then you can have a diet Coke on me at happy hour, along with some of those little barbecue chicken wings. Come on now, give it a try.

7. *Being single, I feel lonely going anywhere for social activities by myself.* Now there's a good reason not to go. It's never fun going alone, but you might meet someone interesting, and maybe a friend will go with you the first time. Who knows, you might meet a number of people who interest you, none of whom you would have met otherwise. Your love life might improve, and good things might follow.

8. *It's more fun to work.* Is it? I doubt it. More than watching a sporting event or going to a musical? More than being outdoors and hiking and seeing and hearing the birds and little varmints you see outdoors? More fun than hearing a good political debate or a lecture on a topic that interests you? Maybe, but I'm skeptical, and from the smile on your face, so are you.

9. *You can't teach an old dog new tricks; or, I am who I am.* Now there's an excuse I hear often. Whoever made that one up gave a lot of people an excuse to stay stuck in life. You aren't an old dog, and there's still plenty to learn, so take advantage of your free time and learn something new. Believe me, if knowledge is power, you have potential to become very powerful, and who knows what good things might follow?

10. *I'm a stay-at-home sort of person.* Baloney. That's just an excuse for not getting out of the house. You know it, and so does everyone else. It's what lonely people say, and it just makes them more lonely in time, so don't use it as an excuse. OK?

Personal Story: Returning to Work

"I retired at 62 after too many years of extremely hard work. I was, truth be told, burned out and dejected that after so many years of very hard work,

I had so little to show for it. I didn't have the acclaim I thought I'd have for the impossible work I did, nor did I have the personal satisfaction. So after some discussion with my daughter, I retired from full-time work. Within three to four months, I missed it . . . a lot. I missed the sense of being part of a university and socializing with smart, nutty, and creative people. I didn't like the loss of status. So I worked part-time for the next five years, always feeling slightly off balance because part-time isn't the same as full-time, and you're not really part of the organization.

"I moved to Prescott, Arizona, from Los Angeles, thinking that I'd probably never teach again, until the nice folks at Arizona State University contacted me. At first they were talking about a full-time job, but that would make it difficult to live in Prescott, a community in the mountains of northern Arizona that's continually touted as one of the best communities in which to retire in America. We settled on one long day a week and courses I really love to teach. The following is a description of the last two years that I've spent teaching graduate school in Phoenix:

"I drive two hours each way from my home to teach courses each semester at a major university. Driving down the mountain from my house in the Arizona backcountry is stunning. You drive by Dead Bug Wash, Black River Canyon, Horse Thief Canyon, and vistas that make you want to hug the scenery. It's a little like you felt as a kid watching a John Wayne movie, only you have a cup of coffee with you and you're listening to a tape by Alison Krauss so beautiful and touching that you want to play it for your students when you see them.

"On the way to class, I stop at the factory outlet stores outside of Phoenix for coffee and find myself buying clothes I need but would never buy because, well, I never thought of myself as someone who wanted to look especially good for others. Academics are just not into clothes. Now that I have some decent clothes to wear, I find myself enjoying the pleasure of dressing well (sort of well, anyway). I've lost a lot of weight, so the pleasure is that much better.

"Once I get to campus, I have a Starbucks coffee in the library, check my e-mail before class, and notice the serious working-class students at a bank of computers. School is no picnic, and most of them work second jobs and sometimes full-time to pay their tuition. It's hard to think that many of them have parents affluent enough to pay their university expenses, yet here they are. It makes me feel optimistic about the future to see such hardworking young people.

"I go to my classes, and although I don't feel I'm as good as I could be because I'm a bit tired from the two hour drive, the students are happy to see me. They've begun to realize that I spend much more time with them than their full-time teachers and that I respond to their e-mails and grade their papers very quickly. Several students have told me that they never get responses from their teachers, and when I respond as soon as they send an e-mail, it's startling, but in a nice way.

"To help me remember lecture material, I audiotape my lectures, play a bit of what I've recorded in class, and then expand on the material. It seems like a good approach, and the students don't seem to mind. I record my lectures the day before classes, in the morning when I'm fresh, and then listen to them in the car while driving to teach. Many times, I tell jokes when I record and find myself laughing at the puns and bad jokes I tell students.

"I've become very good at using the academic Internet program Blackboard and spent a few days with the help of an information technology person learning the mysteries and benefits of that great teaching tool. Because of the long drive, I've decided to offer the occasional Internet class so that certain assignments and examinations can be done online. The students like the freedom, and their work is much improved.

"I make a paltry sum of money for teaching, but the money goes for the frivolous things I never felt comfortable buying before: clothes, a new tennis racket, better tennis shoes, and hiking gear so I can hike these beautiful Arizona mountains. I feel rich with the extra money, and it makes me very generous. I figure that what I make is play money because I get such pleasure from it, so why shouldn't other people benefit?

"I've tried to volunteer, but I'm still tied to the notion that you should be paid for your labor if you are to be valued. I've begun consulting for a new university in my town that will offer a first year of college to young adults in recovery. The money is nice, the work is very interesting, and I feel valued. Between all of that and the books I write, my plate is full. I have time to work out, to hike, and to go to political, cultural, and social events, but the work sustains me and makes me feel that although I'm retired, I'm really still working, but for myself and not for the large organizations that often treat older adults so badly. It's a wonderful feeling, one I dreamed of when I was working full-time at stressful jobs.

"I think work is a necessary part of the aging process. I don't think volunteer work has the same emotional value as paid work, but that's me. And it's not the amount of money I make, it's the fact that I can now focus on what I love doing. There is no amount of money that can equal the feeling of complete independence to pick and choose what excites you.

"It isn't growing old that worries us older people, it's the fear we'll grow old and be bored. To have work that still excites you, that's one of the best rewards. That, and someone who loves you without reservation."—MDG

SUMMARY

This chapter discussed ways of dealing with time following retirement. It included a discussion of why work-addicted people have such difficulty with leisure time as well as discussions of opportunities to pursue new careers, develop new skills through education, part-time work, and consulting. A number of retired people discussed their approach to retirement and some of the problems they initially encountered. Excuses by workaholics for not using leisure time were provided as well as a personal story I wrote about my retirement experiences.

REFERENCES

Heller, K. (1993). Prevention activities for older adults: Social structures and personal competencies that maintain useful social roles. *Journal of Counseling and Development, 72*, 124–130.

Levant, R.F. (1997). The masculinity issue. *Journal of Men's Studies, 5*, 221–229.

Schneider, K.J. (1998). Toward a science of the heart: Romanticism and the revival of psychology. *American Psychologist, 53*, 277–289.

PART VII

Changing Work-
Addicted Behavior

Chapter 16 discusses ways of changing your work-addicted behavior, with special attention paid to the help you can receive from mental health professionals and examples of types of counseling you can expect to get. Chapter 17 contains a few parting words to help you know that it takes time to work retirement out, but once you've done it, retirement can be a very positive and even happy time for many work-addicted people.

CHAPTER 16

Professional Help to Treat Work Addictions

SEEKING PROFESSIONAL HELP

There are many ways in which workaholics can change their behavior. This chapter identifies a few and begins with seeking professional help. The people who provide professional help generally come from the following fields: psychiatry (MD degree), clinical psychology (PhD degree), social work (MSW degree), and counseling (MFCC degree). There is no evidence that one field is better at talking therapy than another. Psychiatrists are the only ones who can prescribe medication. All states require that professionals who provide mental health services be state licensed and have the required amount of experience and education needed to be licensed. This is not so for life coaches, who may not need to be licensed but in fact hold one of the professional mental health degrees noted earlier. Each state has different rules. Your insurance may or may not cover mental health services, although Medicare does, but limits the number of sessions you can attend.

Before going to see a professional, be sure you ask about their rates and whether they accept your insurance. Also, find out about the type of help they provide to determine if you feel comfortable with it. Workaholic behavior isn't always an easy problem to deal with and you'll have to decide how much time and effort you're willing to put into changing your behavior, remembering that not all therapists or approaches to helping suit everyone. Be an informed consumer and approach that person as you would approach a doctor or lawyer by getting as much information and word-of-mouth feedback as possible before you begin counseling. I use the terms *counseling* and *psychotherapy* interchangeably. They are both ways of helping people by discussing their problems. Some therapists use insight, and others are more into advice giving or helping people think through their problem by focusing on irrational elements in their thinking. I'll give a few examples to help you understand the difference.

COUNSELING AND WORKAHOLICS

Workaholics are sometimes not the best candidates for counseling and psychotherapy because a strong streak of independence and denial often defines their approach to their workaholic behavior. Many workaholics are men, and male socialization often values independent solutions to problems that make it difficult for men to seek help. Even when men do seek help, they may not be able to state clearly a relationship between why they feel discomfort and what may be causing it. And because men often grow up believing that others are unable or unwilling to help, or that the process of seeking help is femanizing, they often deal with extreme emotions by themselves.

In discussing male socialization and the assumptions of counseling and psychotherapy, Robertson and Fitzgerald (1992) argue that traditional notions of psychotherapy are often ill suited for men for the following reasons, which also apply to female workaholics: (1) while psychotherapy and counseling require self-awareness, men are encouraged to hide their feelings; (2) counseling and psychotherapy often require people to admit that they have a problem, but men have been taught to deny that they have problems; (3) therapists often encourage clients to share their vulnerabilities, but men have been taught to hide their vulnerabilities so they can maintain a competitive edge; (4) counseling and psychotherapy ask clients to openly explore their problems with another person, but men have often been socialized to distrust others, to maintain rational control over their lives, and to believe that "self-exploration should be done independently and on an intellectual level" (Robertson & Fitzgerald, 1992, p. 241). Given these considerations, it seems reasonable that men avoid a process that requires them to consider failure instead of success, cooperation instead of competition, and vulnerability instead of power.

Cochran and Rabinowitz (2003) argue that people with addictive personalities have been culturally programmed to repress the emotional aspects of their problems. This pertains to all aspects of problems, including those in the workplace; in relationships with children, parents, and siblings; and with intimate relationships.

PROFESSIONAL HELP THAT WORKS

People with addictive personalities often respond positively to help when it is offered in a collaborative way. Gambrill (1999) believes that effective help requires that the counselor and client work together in an equal relationship, in which the client's skills, successes, and intelligence are valued. People respond well to counseling when the counselor understands and appreciates the person. Rather than being critical of their beliefs and attitudes, most people with work addictions want counselors to understand how well they've done in their lives and how successful they've been, even if the results of their success are sometimes problematic.

The following discussion provides examples of the types of professional help that are often effective with work-addicted people.

LIFE COACHING

Life coaching is a brief, goal-oriented way of problem solving that generally works on a specific problem with healthy people for a very limited amount of time. It is highly performance oriented and is much less concerned with the development of insight or broader application to other areas of life. Clients are generally people who have intrusive problems requiring a quick solution. Work-related problems, job changes, divorce work, and relationship problems may all be issues that respond well to coaching.

The characteristics of life coaching that may be useful for work with work-addicted men and women are the following. First, life coaching is geared to here-and-now problems. It doesn't assume that a problem has its origins in the past and tries to find quick, logical solutions. Second, life coaching is very practical. It uses advice, homework, asking other people for information, and searching the Internet and journals for answers to problems. Life coaches often suggest that clients keep logs or write down ideas that are then shared with the coach. This technique seems efficient to many workaholics who believe that taking personal responsibility for change will speed up the process. Third, life coaching encourages the use of behavioral charting to analyze a problem and track success. Charting is a way of problem solving that is familiar to many workaholics. My daughter developed a chart to determine which graduate schools she should focus on when applying to schools in public health. I suggested two or three indicators to determine which schools were most likely to provide a good experience (national rankings, availability of assistantships, and program focus). By the time she sent the chart to me, she had over 20 indicators that helped her determine which schools were best for her. When she was done filling in the information under each indicator, it was clear that four or five programs stood out. My daughter grew up with behavioral charting and feels very comfortable using it. She finds that it cuts down on extraneous efforts to problem solve and that it is very time and energy efficient. Fourth, coaching assumes that clients are emotionally healthy and functioning well but just need some practical and supportive assistance with problem solving. Compare this to counseling and psychotherapy, which assume dysfunction, describe people in unhealthy ways, and often use labels. Finally, coaching is very positive and optimistic. It believes that problems can be resolved in a short period of time and that people have the necessary inner resources and skills to resolve problems with just a little direction from the coach.

An Example. Jane Adler is a strongly work-addicted woman who came to a life coach with concerns about her job performance. Her most recent evaluation was mediocre to poor. Given the company's current economic condition, Jane worried that she might lose her job. With a family to support and no other possibilities of similar work in her field in the community, she was very determined to improve her work performance. The coach looked at her written performance and saw three areas that definitely needed improving. Over two sessions, Jane and the coach worked together on practical ways to improve her performance. They also set up a way of measuring whether improvement was taking place.

After the initial two sessions, Jane sent the coach a weekly progress report by e-mail. Brief telephone calls augmented the reports. Several times, Jane was clearly not following through on the strategies they had decided on, and the coach called her in for a chat about why things didn't seem to be going better and what could be done about it. The coach and client also worked out a "360," a management technique used to get maximum feedback from others about Jane's work performance. With work evaluations coming every three months, they had less than three months to resolve the problem—and they did. The next evaluation placed the client's performance in the low excellent range, and her job was secured.

How did this differ from counseling? Jane had initially gone for therapy as she saw her work evaluations begin to deteriorate. She was also working longer and longer hours but getting little done. The counselor felt that Jane was experiencing a mild depression in response to being passed over for a promotion. There were also some conflicts in the family that seemed to be troubling her and could have been responsible for her poor work performance. Counseling consisted of trying to find out more about her feelings regarding the promotion and her concerns about her family. There were some very good discussions, and the counselor felt that therapy was certainly helping her, until a quarterly evaluation suggested that her performance had slipped even more. Concerned that counseling wasn't helping, Jane sought out the life coach on the advice of some coworkers who had used her in the past with good success. In comparing the two forms of help, Jane said,

I liked both people. I thought they were very competent and caring. I think the counselor was helpful in getting me to talk about my reaction to not getting the promotion and my family problems. She was right in thinking that I was depressed. I was. I just didn't know what to do about work, and she wasn't very helpful.

When I went to the coach, all she talked about was work. I felt there were other things that needed to deal with but that work was the most important thing. She helped a lot. She was very nice in a no-nonsense way, and she knew her stuff. In no time, I was back on track at work but felt there were other issues I needed to deal with before the same thing that happened at work started happening again. So I went back to the therapist, and I'm very happy with the work we're doing together. Why didn't I stay with the coach? I don't know. My life is a lot more complicated than work. I thought I needed someone who would listen and help me figure it all out. I don't think charts and 360s work well for life problems, but maybe they do. I'd recommend a coach for very practical problems and a counselor for more complicated problems. That's my read on it, anyway.

Another Example. In another example of life coaching, Jason Roberts was having problems in his marriage, largely because of workaholism, and went to see a life coach. He explained that he and his wife had been in marital therapy but that they hadn't been able to resolve their problems, and now, facing the prospect of a separation and divorce, he sought some short-term help to prepare himself for the divorce and his new life as an older single man. He shared the following:

The coach was very supportive. He asked what I hoped to accomplish. When I told him, he went to the computer and wrote a contract that specified the problems we would try to resolve. I told him I wanted to feel a lot less stress than I was feeling and to try to deal with the divorce proceedings as calmly and objectively as I could without it affecting my job. I said that my wife was trying to take me to the cleaners and I wanted to come out of the divorce with some money and my ego intact. It was a very business-like experience—sort of like going to a lawyer, I guess. He wrote everything down and read it back to me. When he was done, he asked me to read the contract and, if I agreed, to sign it. It spelled out what I wanted to change and what I had to do to make that happen. It was very logical and straightforward.

I wouldn't say he was very warm, but he was definitely confident and positive, and it sort of set the tone for our work. I went five times, and in that time, we worked out an equitable divorce settlement and spent time trying to lower my stress level. He encouraged walking and other activities and asked me to keep track of my blood pressure and pulse and, if possible, my cholesterol and blood sugars. He also got me to promise that I wouldn't drink during the period when we were trying to figure things out. He said to think of it as if I was in training for a race. The better condition I was in, the better I'd do.

I did very well with the settlement, better than I thought I would. I felt awful about being single, and so we expanded the contract and worked on that. Everything had a solution, he said, I just had to think through the steps of finding the right solution. It was very logical, not very warm, but very successful. I think I went a total of eight times altogether. We went 20 times for marital therapy, and our marriage just got worse and worse. I can't say it was the most memorable experience I've ever had, but it was very successful. Maybe I'll consider therapy down the line if I have any adjustment problems to being single or if I keep putting too much time into work, and maybe I'd go back to see him. I'm just not entirely sure. What I do know is that I came out of this terrible time a lot better than I thought I would, and I'd recommend coaching over therapy for the kind of problem I had. Maybe therapy is better for people who have serious problems, but for practical kinds of problems where you need some advice and direction, I don't think you can beat life coaching.

BRIEF COUNSELING

Brief counseling is a bit like life coaching, only it's more inclusive. It assumes that people are having problems now because of a number of reasons and tries to sort out the major ones and help the person resolve them in 5 to 10 sessions. Most brief counseling uses cognitive therapy, a form of help that tries to get people to understand the irrational things they say to themselves that end up getting them in trouble. I pointed out some irrational things workaholics believe in an earlier chapter. The research says that cognitive therapy is generally very effective with depression and a number of anxiety-related problems. The following example should help you understand how the approach might be applied to work addiction.

An Example. Nelson Byers is a 63-year-old executive of a manufacturing company who had just been told that because the company was facing severe financial problems, he was being given a generous severance package but would no longer have a job. Nelson was experiencing anxiety about the future and depression over the loss of his job well before he thought it was time to retire. Nelson sought out a licensed clinical psychologist who specialized in short-term counseling.

The psychologist explained his approach to Nelson, who thought it made sense. He also said that he expected Nelson to do a good deal of reading and that in any event, he could only provide 10 or fewer sessions. In the type of help he provided, the person receiving help had to do a lot of the work on their own, so Nelson shouldn't expect the psychologist to do it for him. The more Nelson read and asked questions, the sooner he'd stop feeling so badly.

The psychologist asked Nelson to discuss his feelings about the loss of his job. Nelson replied, "I worked my ass off for that company. I put in longer hours than anyone should ever be asked to work, and look what they did to me." The following is a verbatim dialogue between Nelson and the psychologist:

PSYCHOLOGIST: What did they do?

NELSON: They fired me, for God's sake, the SOBs.

PSYCHOLOGIST: So they should have kept you on even though the company is going bankrupt?

NELSON: Well, yeah. I was important. I was a big deal in the company. I should have been one of the last ones to go, not one of the first.

PSYCHOLOGIST: Why do you think you were one of the first?

NELSON: Because the bastards never did appreciate my hard work.

PSYCHOLOGIST:	By hard work, do you mean the number of hours you worked or what you achieved?
NELSON:	Everyone knows that I worked my butt off.
PSYCHOLOGIST:	But you haven't answered the question.
NELSON:	I mean I worked hard. Are you saying it didn't accomplish much?
PSYCHOLOGIST:	I'm asking.
NELSON:	Yeah, you're going to say I was a workaholic, right? Work hard but accomplish little.
PSYCHOLOGIST:	Are you a workaholic?
NELSON:	I've heard that before. Some people thought so.
PSYCHOLOGIST:	What did those people say?
NELSON:	That I worked hard but didn't do much.
PSYCHOLOGIST:	Is it true?
NELSON:	I guess so. You can see what they did to me. They must have thought my work wasn't so red hot.
PSYCHOLOGIST:	But you equate hard work with accomplishment. Might that be a way you approached the job?
NELSON:	I was always very cautious at work. I didn't want to make mistakes.
PSYCHOLOGIST:	In this helping approach I use, we try and figure out the illogical things people tell themselves that get them into trouble. It sounds like you've been telling yourself that the harder you try not to make mistakes, the more you'll control the outcome, but it doesn't lead to better work. It's just a way to protect yourself.
NELSON:	That's what my wife says. She says I can't make decisions and that I always do the most cautious thing possible.
PSYCHOLOGIST:	Who taught you that caution beats risk?
NELSON:	My dad. He never took a risk in his life. He figured the more cautious you were, the more you had control and were vigilant, the better things would be.
PSYCHOLOGIST:	And did it work for him?
NELSON:	He was a failure at everything he ever did, including being a father.
PSYCHOLOGIST:	And you? How would you assess yourself?
NELSON:	Hell, I tried, but my kids hate me and my wife's been talking divorce after 35 years of marriage. I guess you could say I haven't been so successful, but at least I made better money than the old man, and I had higher status.
PSYCHOLOGIST:	That's certainly something to be proud of, but as you move to this next stage in your life, might it be good to think through the

	strategies of caution that you've used at work with the many extra hours you put in to make certain everything was controlled for and perhaps use some different strategies, particularly as they relate to your family?
NELSON:	Looks like I'll have lots of time to be with my family if they'll let me. What should I tell them?
PSYCHOLOGIST:	Were it me, I'd explain what you did at work, and why, and how you know it pushed them away from you, and that you apologize from the bottom of your heart and want to make things a lot better.
NELSON:	You don't think they'll laugh at me?
PSYCHOLOGIST:	Would you laugh knowing what you've just gone through at work?
NELSON:	No, I surely wouldn't.

The psychologist gave Nelson some material to read about cautious and controlling behavior as well as the type of counseling he was using, which was called *cognitive therapy*. He asked Nelson to read the articles and e-mail back his take on the material and how it applied to him. At first, Nelson used excuses or gave feedback that was intelligent but didn't really apply to him. Nelson also had trouble accepting his own involvement for the job loss and kept blaming the company. However, after a few sessions, he got down to work and started understanding his own involvement in the problems at work. He also had a family session, and much to his amazement and surprise, his family was very understanding. Nelson broke down and cried during the family meeting. For the first time in a long time, he felt the deep connection he once had with his children and wife. It was a very moving experience for him.

Nelson has enough money to retire early and live well, but he wants to continue working. Over the years he has developed a network of colleagues, and after contacting them, many of them also the victims of the recession, they banded together as a cooperative, and after six months of working at it, now Nelson has enough work to keep him occupied. He struggles with putting too much time into making things perfect so he won't make mistakes, but he's doing better, and his wife helps. They've agreed that no matter what, Nelson will have dinner with his family every night, go to social and cultural functions together, and never work on Sundays, which is a designated family day.

In a follow-up meeting with his therapist, Nelson said, "You introduced me to a new way of thinking. I had a hard time with it at first because it was a lot more comfortable to keep doing what I always did: throw work at any problem. I'm not sure any workaholic can ever say that he's really happy, but I keep pinching myself to make sure I'm telling the truth, and you know what? I *am* happy."

SUPPORT GROUPS

Support or self-help groups, as they are also known, "consist of individuals who share the same problem or concern. Members provide emotional support to one another, learn ways to cope, discover strategies for improving their condition, and help others while helping themselves " (Wituk, Shepherd, Slavich, Warren, & Meissen, 2000, p. 157). The authors indicate that an estimated 25 million Americans have been involved in self-help groups at some point during their lives. Positive outcomes have been found in groups treating substance abuse (Humphreys & Moos, 1996), bereavement (Caserta & Lund, 1993), caregiving (McCallion & Toseland, 1995), diabetes (Gilden, Hendryx, Clar, Casia, & Singh, 1992), and depression (Kurtz, 1990, 1997). Riessman (2000) reports that "more Americans try to change their health behaviors through self-help than through all other forms of professional programs combined" (p. 47).

Riessman and Carroll (1995) identify the following principles defining the function and purpose of self-help groups:

1. Members share a similar condition and understand each other.
2. Members determine activities and policies that make self-help groups very democratic and self-determining.
3. Helping others is therapeutic.
4. Self-help groups build on the strengths of the individual members, the group, and the community; charge no fees; and are not commercialized.
5. Self-help groups function as a social support system that helps participants cope with traumas through supportive relationships between members.
6. Values are projected that define the true meaning of the group to its members.
7. Self-help groups use the expertise of members to help one another.
8. Seeking assistance from a self-help group is not as stigmatizing as seeking help from a mental health provider.
9. Self-help groups focus on the use of self-determination, inner strength, self-healing, and resilience.

An Example. Leonard Bayers is a 63-year-old attorney suffering from chronic depression that has lasted almost five years and began when his wife of 30 years passed away. Leonard has had problems with work addiction much of his life, and since his wife passed away, he has been working 100 hours or more a week. Leonard is being seen by a psychiatrist to monitor his antidepression medication and has been in therapy with a clinical psychologist for almost five years. The medication and therapy have had a negligible impact on his depression and his work addiction. Leonard is too depressed to exercise and has become a compulsive eater, with almost 75 pounds gained over the past five years. His therapist suggested a self-help group for people with chronic depression as an adjunct to therapy and medication, but Leonard has been unwilling to attend meetings, believing that the group will be as unsuccessful as his current treatment. The therapist arranged for Leonard to meet with the group leader, someone who, like Leonard, fights chronic depression but has successfully learned to cope with it.

The leader invited Leonard to attend a meeting and asked participants to stay after so they could honestly discuss their feelings about the group and to answer questions Leonard might have about the group's effectiveness. The group leader also shared some research that the national chapter of the group had accumulated. Over 70 percent of the participants who stayed in the group more than two years reported fewer missed days at work, fewer doctor's visits, decreased use of antidepressants, and fewer days of depression. The average length of depression before the respondents began their group participation was more than five years. Participants who stayed with the group two years or longer had better results than those who discontinued involvement before completing a full year of group participation. Those who dropped out of the group early cited personality clashes with the group leader and differences of opinion about the purpose of the group as the major reasons for attrition.

Leonard decided to give the group a try and began attending sessions on a regular basis, while also seeing his therapist weekly and continuing with his antidepression medication. After six months as a participant, Leonard told the therapist about the experience:

It's very supportive. Everyone there is like me. They're all older people struggling with depression. Some of them, like me, overwork to deal with loneliness. A few have lost their spouses, and many of us realize we've always felt lonely and isolated and use coping methods like overworking, compulsive eating, and drinking to deal with our unhappiness. The difference is that they get on with their lives. That's what I've begun doing. I've been assigned a woman about my age as a mentor, who I call when I feel so down I can't function. We've begun walking together, and it's helped me lose weight. I feel a lot of positive acceptance from the other people, and that helps a lot. We have speakers who talk about depression and who keep us informed about the latest research. I've been assigned as a mentor to a new member, and surprisingly, he seems to find a lot of solace from our contact.

I still feel really depressed, but while it used to be everyday, now I have good and bad days. Overall, I think I'm less depressed than I was before I started the group. Mainly, I think the support, the camaraderie, the loving environment, and the sense that we're all experts on depression and have something to say worth listening to are what helps the most. I've made a couple of good friends from the group, and instead of staying home and being lonely and working, I go out to movies or have dinner with my friends. It helps from feeling lonely, which is one of the things depressed people often experience. Do I feel better than I did six months ago? Yes. Is it because of the group? I think some of it is, but I have to admit that because of the group, I'm using therapy better. So overall, yes, I give it high marks. I'll stay with it, and maybe in time, I'll be able to get by without any help at all. That's my goal, for sure.

GUIDED READING

Many people learn to use the Internet to gather information about emotional problems. The purposes of finding information about one's problems are (1) to provide information, (2) to gain insight, (3) to find solutions, (4) to stimulate discussion of problems, (5) to suggest new values and attitudes, and (6) to understand how others have coped with problems similar to their own (Pardeck, 1995).

Novels, poetry, music, films, and videos can also be particularly useful because they often depict issues that many of us are trying to resolve in our own lives (e.g., problems with children, problems at work, relationship problems, and problems with drinking and other addictions).

When I work with clients, I help them find articles online that will give them some understanding of their problem and will also help them resolve it. I try to use articles that are written in a clear and understandable way. Many professional articles are written for other professionals and are difficult to understand if you have no background or training in the mental health professions.

An Example. Jenny Blair is a 62-year-old accountant and workaholic. She works 80 hours a week and sometimes more. The amount of work she gets done isn't at all in keeping with the number of hours she works, and Jenny has begun to realize that much of the time she puts into her work is wasted. She doesn't understand this at all, and the anger her long hours have produced in her husband threatens their marriage. I helped Jenny find a number of useful articles about workaholics. One in particular about perfectionism hit a chord in Jenny, and she began to talk about her perfectionistic mother, who was also fearful and anxious much of the time. Jenny wondered to what extent her mother's perfectionism had affected her. The more articles she found on her own, the more she was able to self-diagnose and treat the problem. She told me,

I've always been able to figure out what to do when I have a problem, but in the past five years, as I get closer to retirement, I've begun putting in many more hours than are needed to do the work. The articles I read suggested that this was a form of anxiety and that letting go of work is difficult for many people as they get older. I guess many of us start wondering if we're going to be useless when we stop working. I found the articles very helpful, and talking about them with my counselor sort of helped me use the information in the articles to focus on my problems.

I found many articles just using the search term "workaholic" on Google. I also used terms like "perfectionists" and "adult anxiety." Once I got proficient at using the Internet, I was able to use my husband's website at his work, which allowed me to read professional articles on a browser called EbsoHost, a social science and psychology search engine. I also found good material on Psych Abstracts. Some of the articles were a bit difficult to understand, but my husband, who's a statistician, helped me out. Knowing that I was trying to do something to help myself really motivated him to help me.

Counseling is usually just 50 minutes long once a week. That doesn't mean you can't do some work when you're away from counseling. I did, and what was a really upsetting and intrusive problem began to resolve itself in less than 10 weeks. I think that's pretty good considering how nutty I was getting and how angry my husband was starting to get. I work normal hours now and enjoy my marriage, and I'm actively looking forward to retiring in a few years. I've worked hard all my life, and I deserve some quality time. I may work part-time or I may not. Right now it just feels good to be normal again.

SUMMARY

This chapter offered suggestions and examples of how work-addicted people can get professional help to reduce and eliminate their work-addictive behavior. The several approaches suggested included life coaching, brief counseling, support groups, and selective reading. A description of the professionals who offer services and their degrees was also included in the chapter along with examples from people who have used mental health professionals to resolve their work addictions.

REFERENCES

Caserta, M.S., & Lund, D.A. (1993). Intrapersonal resources and the effectiveness of self-help groups for bereaved older adults. *Gerontologist, 33*, 619–629.

Cochran, S.V. and Rabinowitz, F.E. (2003). Gender-sensitive recommendations for assessment and treatment of depression in men. *Professional Psychology: Research and Practice, 34*, 132–140.

Gambrill, E. (1999). Evidence-based practice: An alternative to authority-based practice. *Journal of Contemporary Human Services, 80*, 341–350.

Gilden, J.L., Hendryx, A.S., Clar, S., Casia, P., & Singh, S.P. (1992). Diabetes support groups improve health care of older diabetic patients. *Journal of the American Geriatrics Society, 40*, 147–150.

Humphreys, K., & Moos, R.H. (1996). Reduced substance-abuse-related health care costs among voluntary participants in Alcoholics Anonymous. *Psychiatric Services, 47*, 709–713.

Kurtz, L.F. (1990). The self-help movement: Review of the past decade of research. *Social Work with Groups, 13*(3), 101–115.

Kurtz, L.F. (1997). *Self-help and support groups: A handbook for practitioners*. Thousand Oaks, CA: Sage Publications.

McCallion, P., & Toseland, R.W. (1995). Supportive group interventions with caregivers of frail older adults. *Social Work with Groups, 18*(1), 11–25.

Pardeck, J.T. (1995). Bibliotherapy: An innovative approach for helping children. *Early Childhood Development and Care, 110*, 83–88.

Riessman, F. (2000). Self-help comes of age. *Social Policy, 30*(4), 47–49.

Riessman, F., & Carroll, D. (1995). *Redefining self-help: Policy and practice*. San Francisco: Jossey-Bass.

Robertson, J.M., & Fitzgerald, L.F. (1992). The mistreatment of men: Effects of client gender role and life style on diagnosis and attrition on pathology. *Journal of Counseling Psychology, 39*, 240–246.

Wituk, S., Shepherd, M.D., Slavich, S., Warren, M.L., & Meissen, G. (2000). A topography of self-help groups: An empirical analysis. *Social Work, 45*, 157–165.

CHAPTER 17

Final Words

No one ever said that retirement is easy. It isn't, but even the most work-addicted among you can find peace and achieve many of the great things you'd always hoped for in retirement. With more and more people living healthy lives well into their 90s and beyond, you have a great deal of time to find out what you really want to do and then do it. As my daughter keeps reminding me, life isn't a race, but before you can come to appreciate what that means, you need to take some time to get to know what you really want.

The management expert Frederick Hertzberg said that when you ask people if they're satisfied with their jobs, almost 100 percent of them say they are. If you ask again, 100 percent of them say "yes, but," and if you ask the same question seven times, the answer you get is often, "No, but it was the best thing I could find at the time, and it's offered me the ability to raise a family. Would I want my kids to do what I do? Absolutely not."

That means that before you retire, and even after you retire, you need to do some soul searching and ask yourself tough questions you may not want to ask. It's no crime to be a workaholic. We're the ones who make the railroads run on time and the nation work. But after years of giving your all to someone else, it's time to give your all to you.

I look back on my life, and yes, I've achieved a lot, but so what? I don't live in the past, and neither do you. The question is, what are you going to do with yourself today, tomorrow, and the day after? Knowing the answer takes time and effort. It's never too soon to ask yourself that question and to do some practicing to see if your solutions work. You've put your heart and soul into solving problems. This is a problem you can solve. If you can't, there are plenty of people among your family, friends, and professionals who can help. Don't think that if you can't figure it out, the answer will come magically to you after you retire. It won't.

It may be that your answer is a mix of work, more family involvement, volunteering, and constructive use of leisure time to stay healthy and involved with friends. Or you can keep on working full-time, if at all possible, and let the answer come to you as you begin to reach that moment in time when you don't feel like working full-time any longer. But think about it, and practice the behaviors you want to add to your life.

Am I optimistic that you'll enjoy retirement? Yes, but it takes a lot of time and a lot of work. I hope you do the work well before you retire, but if you're like many of your fellow workaholics, you might not. What then? What if you find yourself without a job before you're ready to retire because the job market has gone south and your company or organization is in deep financial trouble and is laying off older workers? Then use your talents to figure out what comes next in your life. That's why I wrote this book: to help you develop a retirement plan and to be proactive so that other people don't control your fate.

And don't be unrealistic about retirement. You'll have bad days when you're bored, just as you have bad days when you work. So what? The trick is to have lots of good days but to accept the ones that aren't so great as part of the human condition. If you think everyone is always happy, look around and see if you can find many people who are always happy. I don't. I listen to my fellow coffee drinkers when I take my dog for coffee, and yes, many of them are happy, but the ones who aren't—and there are many of them, old and young—sound unhappy in a way that all of us are unhappy. We don't feel well. Our relationships aren't good. A friend isn't being a friend. A loved one isn't being as loving as we'd like them to be. That's life before and after retirement.

You have time now to do the great deeds, to find what makes you truly happy. Teddy Roosevelt said it best in his speech "Citizenship in a Republic" (Sorbonne, Paris, April 23, 1910):

It is not the critic who counts: not the man who points out how the strong man stumbles or where the doer of deeds could have done better. The credit belongs to the man who is actually in the arena, whose face is marred by dust and sweat and blood, who strives valiantly, who errs and comes up short again and again, because there is no effort without error or shortcoming, but who knows the great enthusiasms, the great devotions, who spends himself for a worthy cause; who, at the best, knows, in the end, the triumph of high achievement, and who, at the worst, if he fails, at least he fails while daring greatly, so that his place shall never be with those cold and timid souls who knew neither victory nor defeat.

So good luck, my fellow workaholics. We form a community of doers and achievers. Let me know how you're doing. If you need help, I'm always happy to give suggestions and advice. You can contact me through my Web site (http://www.morleyglicken.com/), or at mglicken@msn.com and I'm always happy to respond.

Personal Story: Working Full-Time While Flying Round-Trip between a Foreign Country and America

"My name is David Naiditch. I'm 68 years old, and I've been happily married for over 30 years. I'm the father of eight children, six with my current wife and two by a former marriage. I'm close to my children and consider myself an involved and caring father. I'm also a religious person and practice a form of Judaism that is very orthodox. I'm currently the general manager of Paratransit Transportation System, which contracts with Miami-Dade County, Florida, to provide transportation for the disabled under the requirements of the Americans with Disabilities Act. I've been working in Miami for 10 years and have been in the same line of work for 28 years, in the Twin Cities, Dallas, Boston, and now Miami. I've been able to achieve a high level of success even though I only have a high school education. I feel vital and alive and, like many people, I'm still trying to figure out what I want to be when I grow up.

"I love to work. Many people think I'm a workaholic, but I don't. Work gives me pleasure, and I'm good at what I do. I never think of work as a chore but rather as something that requires skill and uses a number of complex abilities I know that I have. When I work, I feel alive and in use of all my faculties. However, I really don't love my job. I manage a system where we have a government contract. The bureaucracy and paperwork keep getting worse every year. In addition, everybody seems to exercise their rights, and we have to deal with employees who claim discrimination and unequal treatment. All in all, work is not as fun as it used to be. In fact, it is downright aggravating half the time, between our clients and our employees. Again, I tolerate the situation because I need to keep busy and to make enough money to continue my lifestyle and to help some of my married children financially. I often read that this is the first time in several generations where the children won't have it better than their parents. That certainly is true of my children, who work hard and are responsible and caring people but need some additional help to make it. I would hate to be starting out now.

"Three years ago, I decided that I wanted to live in Israel, particularly the northern part overlooking the Mediterranean Sea. I was in Israel in 1971 and went on a tour to Nahariya, Israel, which is on the Mediterranean Sea six miles south of the Lebanese border, and fell in love with the place. Nahariya is a small city of about 52,000, within walking distance of everything and a two-hour train ride to the airport in Tel Aviv. The second time I made a visit to the area in 1995, I decided that I wanted to live there someday.

"That day came in 2007 when I made arrangements through the Internet with a real estate agency that had a franchise with an American company. I flew to Israel from Miami, and three of my children who were living in Israel and going to school there came along with me, and we looked at seven or eight condos. The agent saved the best one for last. The apartment was in a 13-unit building on the fourth floor with a view overlooking the Mediterranean and a wraparound penthouse balcony. The unit is 1,400 square feet, which may be small by American standards, but it has four bedrooms, two bathrooms with showers, and the view along with the sea breezes made it the one I chose. I did a walk-around, checked for creaks and leaks, and decided that I'd found the right place. I met the realtor the next morning for breakfast, made an offer, the owners counteroffered, and we had a deal.

"Now I had two challenges. The first was to inform my wife what I did—she had told me not to buy anything—and the second challenge was how to pay for it. I had agreed to make monthly payments for 10 months, even though we were still living in Miami and had been trying to sell our house for 6 months without a single offer and with prices dropping every day. This was in November 2007, when the real estate bubble was starting to burst. With some convincing, my wife agreed that living in Israel would be pretty wonderful, and she agreed to buy the condo and move to Israel.

"Thankfully, I'd started taking out life insurance policies when I was only 14 years old and borrowed the money to purchase my new home until the Miami home sold—it's called a swing loan. Finally, in July 2008, our home sold at about 40 percent less than we were originally asking.

"The next hurdle was informing the group of four individuals who own the company I work for. I arranged a luncheon meeting for the five of us at a quiet kosher restaurant. At that time we had about 18 months remaining on our five-year contract. After I ordered appetizers and we each had a glass of wine, I took out a folded sheet of paper with my talking points. I then informed the group—two men and two women—about my plan to move to Israel at the end of August 2008 and that I wanted to work 10 days a month in Miami and live in Israel for 20 days a month. I would commute between Israel and Miami once a month. The two women ran outside and cried, and the two men were just angry. Their comment was that we had 18 months on the contract remaining, and why couldn't I just stay until the end of the contract and put together a new contract before I left?

"I had been with the group as general manager for nine years, and we had gone through a successful rebid of the contract in 2004. Fortunately, I'm very good at putting together proposals. Over the years, I've been successful at making a good deal of money for the company.

"The major owner proposed that I work 20 days a month in Miami and then take off 10 days a month to live in Israel. I told him that life was too short and that I really wanted to do my original plan of 10 days in Miami and 20 in Israel, enjoying casual time and sitting on my deck overlooking the Mediterranean Sea with a beer in my hand, but I told him I would think about it and that we would talk later.

"A week later, I met with the major owner, who is a very convincing person, and I agreed to work about three weeks a month in Miami and take 11 to 14 days off in Nahariya. Also, I proposed that I take a 25 percent cut in pay, with the company paying for business-class airline tickets. I have a bad back, and the extra comfort of having larger, more comfortable seats was important to me.

"The next step was to sign up for Social Security benefits. I waited the extra year and began receiving benefits at 66 years and eight months of age. What a disappointment! At that time I had earned enough that my annual salary for the last 20 years had the maximum amount taken from my earnings for Social Security. So after the $450 or so that is taken for Medicare, my current monthly check is $2,229. In addition, I am taxed on that amount as ordinary income. My wife has another year or so to go before she will receive about $700 a month. The combination of the two Social Security payments is just not enough to live on. By working at 75 percent of my salary, even with the travel and the cost of having a small apartment in Miami, I'm in a much better place financially.

"I never really had an IRA because all our children were sent to private schools. I had a deferred income plan with the management company I worked for to manage the contract in Miami, but a little over three years ago, they severed the contract with my owners. This resulted in my having to take the money they paid into my deferred income plan and roll all of it over into a tax-deferred IRA plan with a mix of stocks and bonds that was supposed to be conservative. The market was good then, and I thought I would be OK. Like the rest of us, my IRA is down about 40 percent from my original investment, which has made continued work absolutely necessary.

"So where am I now after my 15th 14,000-mile round trip between Miami and Israel? Thomas Friedman wrote a best seller called *The World Is Flat*. It really is. To help me stay in touch with my office in Miami when I'm in Israel, I have high-speed Internet service, scanners, and cell phones I can use in America and Israel. The main problem is that when I'm not in Miami, I miss the easiness of just walking down the hall to someone's office or getting in my car when I need to speak face-to-face with a client or associate. A general manger needs direct, face-to-face contact with people. I am considering Skype conference calling.

"The contract that was supposed to be expiring in March 2010 is now being extended to October 1, 2010, making my original 18 months of flying back and forth a full two years. I hope that we will be the successful bidder on the new contract, which is scheduled to begin in October 2010.

"The most difficult part of my situation is the loneliness I experience when I return to Miami Beach. My wife and I have been married for almost 35 years and have always had an excellent relationship. I am able to have her return with me to Miami three times a year, but that still means that I'm alone nine 21-day periods out of the year, or 189 days a year. I'm renting a studio apartment in Miami with about 350 square feet and two small windows. The trade-off for continuing to work and being financially able to live where I'd always wanted to live is being alone a lot. At my age, loneliness is painful.

"My other problem is that I don't qualify for the Israel National Health Insurance system because I am in and out of the country once a month. I have to be in the country for 183 days in a year to establish residency before I am eligible. This could pose a big problem if I require medical attention outside the United States during the 183-day waiting period because Medicare doesn't cover out-of-country medical expenses. For the time I'm in Israel, I don't have medical coverage.

"The Israeli health insurance system is quite good because you have a choice of four to five plans, and they all have three levels of coverage. You can also have a choice of doctors in the plan, make appointments online, and get the results of any tests without having to speak to someone.

"I went to a doctor who saw me as a private-pay patient, and it cost me the equivalent of $175. The good news is that my prescriptions for Coumadin—I have a bad heart valve—and Zalatan eyedrops for glaucoma cost about two-thirds of the price that I pay in America under my secondary insurance with Aetna.

"Other than that, we don't have a car yet in Israel, so I walk about four to five miles per day, which is quite enjoyable. Both the stationary and the walking scenery is very pleasant to look at. The food is healthy and nourishing. Overall, I feel good.

"We both passed our driver's test, which was quite a feat. Even though I have been driving for 50 years and am a National Safely Council instructor, I had to take 13 driving lessons, but I passed the driving test the first time. My wife passed hers the second time. The rules and signs are much different than in the United States. I know of people who have taken the test nine times.

"Another issue is the devaluation of American currency. The exchange rate has decreased by over 8 percent this year, and there is no end in sight. This means that our American dollar buys 8 percent less in Israel than it did last year and may continue to fall. It's a real issue for anyone planning to move to another country.

"My plan is to continue my current arrangement for as long as I can physically travel back and forth. My company appreciates my work and the money that I help them make. It takes me about 17 hours door-to-door traveling between Miami and Nahariya and about 20 hours on the return leg of the trip. In addition, I am awake about 40 hours each way, and I'm never able to sleep on the plane, although I read a lot and listen to books on tape.

"It was destiny that they talked me into working longer each month. I certainly need the money, and being able to spend quality time in Israel and see the beauty and experience the spirituality of the country is something I can't translate into money terms. One can really feel the holiness of the country, even though many of the residents are not observant. It's in the air, on the land, and with the people. It makes my hard work and the long flights back and forth worthwhile. Only the future knows how long I can continue doing this, but for the time being, I'm happy to have a well-paying job and to live a lifestyle I find meaningful. During a time when older people are having such difficulty making it at all, that's saying something."—David Naiditch, Miami, Florida, and Nahariya, Israel

Index

About the Author

DR. MORLEY D. GLICKEN is the former dean of the Worden School of Social Service in San Antonio; the founding director of the Master of Social Work Department at California State University, San Bernardino; the past director of the Master of Social Work Program at the University of Alabama; and the former executive director of Jewish Family Service of Greater Tucson. He has also held faculty positions in social work at the University of Kansas and Arizona State University. He currently teaches in the Department of Social Work at Arizona State University in Tempe.

Dr. Glicken received his BA degree in social work with a minor in psychology from the University of North Dakota and the holds a Master of Social Work degree from the University of Washington and Master of Public Administration and Doctor of Social Work degrees from the University of Utah. He is a member of Phi Kappa Phi Honorary Fraternity.

Dr. Glicken has published numerous books, including the following: *A Simple Guide to Retirement* (with Brian Haas; Praeger, 2009); *Evidence-Based Practice with Troubled Children and Adolescents: A Psychosocial Perspective* (Elsevier, 2009); *Evidence Based Counseling and Psychotherapy with an Aging Population* (Elsevier, 2009); *A Guide to Writing for Human Service Professionals* (Rowman and Littlefield, 2008); *Life Lessons from Resilient People* (Sage, 2006); *Working with Troubled Men: A Practitioner's Guide* (Lawrence Erlbaum Associates, 2005); *Improving the Effectiveness of the Helping Professions: An Evidence-Based Approach to Practice* (Sage, 2004); *Violent Young Children* (Allyn and Bacon/Longman, 2003); *Understanding and Using the Strengths Perspective* (Allyn and Bacon/Longman, 2003); *The Role of the Helping Professions in the Treatment of Victims and Perpetrators of Crime* (with Dale Sechrest; Allyn and Bacon/Longman, 2002); and *A Simple Guide to Social Research* (Allyn and Bacon/Longman, 2002).

Dr. Glicken has published over 50 articles in professional journals and has written extensively on personnel issues for Dow Jones, the publisher of the *Wall Street Journal*. He has held clinical social work licenses in Alabama and Kansas. He is currently Professor Emeritus in Social Work at California State University, San Bernardino, and Executive Director of the Institute for Personal Growth: A Research, Treatment, and Training Institute in Prescott, Arizona, which offers consulting services in counseling, research, and management.

More information about Dr. Glicken may be obtained by visiting his Web site (http://www.morleyglicken.com). A listing of all of his books may be found on Amazon.com (https://authorcentral.amazon.com/v/1973805540), and he can be contacted by e-mail at mglicken@msn.com.